Germany's Fourth Reich

Origins and Development
Seeking World Domination
Commanding EU
Diminishing Britain

by

Harry Beckhough

The June Press

First published in 2004
Re-print with updates 2008
Reprint 2014

by The June Press Ltd

UK distributor
The June Press Ltd
PO Box 119, Totnes
Devon TQ9 7WA
Tel: 44(0)8456 120 175
Email: info@junepress.com
Web: www.junepress.com

Copyright © Harry Beckhough 2014

All rights reserved. No part of this publication may be reproduced or transmitted in any form or by any means of electronic or mechanical, including photocopy, recording, or any information storage and retrieval system now known or invented, without permission in writing from the publisher, except by a reviewer who wishes to quote brief passages in connection with a review written for inclusion in a magazine, newspaper or broadcast.

ISBN 978-0-9927501-1-4

June Press publications are not intended to represent a corporate view of developments in Europe. They are to promote and develop ideas and encourage individuals to express views on all subjects, within the security and obligations of a stable and law-abiding nation. The views expressed in our publications are the sole responsibility of the authors.

Contents

Acknowledgements	i
Foreword	1
Germany's First Reich	5
Germany's Second Reich	8
Germany's Third Reich	12
Germany's Fourth Reich - The New Beginning	19
The Plot Continues	24
Expanding by Ratchets	27
Key Features of German Deceit	36
Bundeswehr	46
The Bertelsmann Group	48
U.S.A.	57
Soviet Russia's Planned EU	62
History	64
Angela Merkel & Her Con/Treaty	68

Acknowledgements

The Bible: Pentateuch

Encyclopaedia Britannica

Sir Winston Churchill (my inspiration)

Nietzsche and the philosophers

Gerald Flurry

Ron Fraser

Lindsay Jenkins

Bernard Connolly

Christopher Story

R E M Francis (PC guidance)

And international historians and observers of the German eternal threat to world peace.

Foreword

Dear Reader,
"My critical analysis of 2003 now completely sold out of further reprints, I am urged to produce a more up-to-date version, illustrating the stages of entrapment in the present Con/Treaty, finally closing the net, after Brown's refusal of Blair's promised Referendum. Thus ending the series of lies from our trusted, elected leaders since 1972; the negation of all that my generation was brought up to believe in, King, Country and People. Sovereignty and Freedom under our own laws and rights from Magna Carta and Bill of Rights, fought and won by worthy forbears. All that had been loyally upheld, unconquerable, including those two World Wars, in which we defended Britain and the rest of the World from the ever- aggressive onslaught of Germany's costly attempts to gain mastery of Europe, under Kaiser Wilhelm and Hitler in turn: Costly in terms also of lives of mothers and children, in the Nazis vain attempt to bomb them into terrified surrender.

We, who lived, fought and sacrificed through the worst two wars ever perpetrated by Germany's aggressive, brutal leaders, can never forget the unspeakable horrors of those repeated German wilful attempts to conquer and rule Europe and most of the world. Britain, never defeated since the eleventh century, stands now on the brink of final betrayal by enemies and traitors and misguided, bedazzled,' hooked' converts within. Beginning with PM Heath, who persuaded the trusting people of Britain who had elected him in good faith and belief in his sworn oath and promises, to accept his lies and deceit in inducing us into what he falsely portrayed as 'only a Common Market for sale and exchange of goods with the people of Europe, to our mutual benefit.' What he sold us, with his tissue of lies, was not a bill of goods, but the forfeiture of our sovereignty and hard-won freedom, for his mess of pottage.

Those lies, which cheated his trusting people into the devised traps of the European Union, led by the tricksters of Germany and France, had him signing away the rights and living of our loyal fishermen and farmers (major food suppliers, without whom we might well have lost the war), have been continued by successive leaders ever since. Sole exception our best post-war Prime Minister Margaret Thatcher, who discovered this devilishly clever deception, led by some of her own Ministers, and publicly proclaimed "NO, NO, NO, in her famous outburst at Bruges, exposing the conspiracy. They then plotted her downfall in guilty revenge. Such are the machinations of these top-level supporters of EU. So it has continued ever since, always with the same objective as planned craftily by EU, led more and more strongly by Germany, with now junior partner France, to the detriment of Britain, gradually being deprived of her erstwhile strength Treaty after Treaty, removing our freedom and liberty, stage by stage, until culmination, revealing the carefully prepared so-called Constitution, which finally transforms us into obedient servants of a German-led embryo dictatorship, on communist lines.

As a language student in Germany in 1933, I witnessed Hitler's meteoric vault to Power, and heard his semi-hysterical speeches, rousing the masses. Then savage assaults by brutal, bullying Nazi Brownshirts and even more menacing cold-blooded, merciless behaviour of his chosen bodyguard the black-clad SS executioners. I was dismayed to hear German philosophers like Heidegger at Freiburg University and Bertrand at Cologne, writing and speaking in praise of Hitler, almost as a Wagnerian hero. Returning home, I had the pleasure of personal discussions with Winston Churchill, then Chancellor of Bristol University, who presented me with my degrees. I became his devoted follower, especially after his tremendous speech as "The Voice in the Wilderness." Deprived of all his offices, and finally relegated to the Back Benches by PM Chamberlain, cast aside by the appeasers and Nazi and Mussolini fascist supporters, they failed to stop his determined, continuous warnings of Hitler's intentions.

Next, my War service in India, then transfer to Intelligence and Bletchley Park, to become Code-breaker, first with 8th Army Desert Campaign, deciphering Rommel's ciphers and campaign dispatches, with translation for Montgomery, who claimed he could "read Rommel's mind". Followed by similar service with the 14th (Burma) Army against the Japanese. Finally, Foreign Office remit to reopen and resuscitate the war-damaged German Rhineland Universities of Cologne and Bonn, from end 1945 to end of 1950. There I met and became friendly with Dr. Konrad Adenauer, former Oberbürgermeister (elected Lord Mayor) of Cologne.

I mollified 'Adi' during his frequent visits to my warm office in the University (freezing outside), with real coffee (only 'ersatz' (artificial) obtainable generally, except on the Schwarze Markt (Black Market), and Schnapps. My friendly office was quite popular, helping 'defensive' visitors relax and speak openly. Reminding him that he was Head of CDU (Christian Democratic Party) and most likely to become the first post-war

German Chancellor – after Hitler – he smiled and said "Haben Sie irgend eine Ahnung was das heisst?" (Have you the slightest idea of the burden that entails?). He regarded me as a harmless, helpful academic with fluent German saying they were grateful for my work in restoring Cologne University (cf my reports to Foreign Office), so he talked to me in confidence, as did his sister at Council meetings. The family home was in Bonn, hence his choice of this very small town as German Capital, in place of Berlin, badly damaged and in 4-Party control, especially Russian enclave.

Adenauer confided some of his plans for restoration of his Germany's rightful pride and world regard. It was an open secret, how many leading Nazis had escaped Underground from end 1943 to 1945, with the help of Vatican 'rat' lines. In confidence Adenauer told me of his good reception in America, where he was skilfully able to massage their fears of a Communist uprising in Western Europe, by authoritatively claiming that he was the only one capable of dealing first-hand with Russians via Berlin. He persuaded the Americans that he was fully aware of the rising Communist menace (which in truth did not exist), and could deal with it best with American support. They believed him implicitly (our trusting West is just not brought up to pierce and dissect the wholesale lies and cunning deceit, of which both Russians and Germans are so adept). Hence the outpouring of cascades of American dollars into Adenauer's lap when, in fact, Intelligence colleagues found only small traces of Communism.

Actually, he was in regular contact both with the Russians with whom he was on good terms, and with the Nazi underground through their International H.Q. at Madrid. In fact he was already employing up to 150 'returnees' in his Ministry. He knew how to play both sides equally well, and how to bring the French on board, with support of de Gaulle and the host of small French farmers. He laid the foundation of Germany's speedy restoration in power and influence by the 1950s. They simply take defeat in their stride, and quickly begin expanding frontiers and rebuilding Baltic strength.

My personal experiences, inspired my research in depth, seeking the thread running continuously through the German mindset and their closeness to the hedonist Russian world of lies and deceit, carried on by KGB after 1990/91 collapse, with arch deceivers like Yeltsin, and especially Gorbachëv, who successfully tricked the Western world – as revealed by Christopher Story, and others. I foresee, with confidence, that their latest, and far too speedily advanced effort at domination and dictatorship of greater Europe, East and West, is also doomed to end in chaos, with the final break-up and dissolution of the now almost totally German-led, oversized EU, Especially with the growing inner-European scepticism, as truth gradually emerges of its hollow, lying, manic structure and total mismanagement of accounts, with billions missing through perpetual robbery, deceit and cheating. A long series of accountants have all refused to accept and sign of the accounts. The incoming new members have refused to accept the Franco-German conditions of entry. Member states cheat regularly with their consumption returns, claiming billions of Euros in false claims.

Yet our own political leaders still refuse to open their eyes and their minds to the truth. They still maintain the medicine will be "good for us", however bitter the taste. That we are better within the demonic heat of the EU, than withdrawing to the confident rebuild of our own lost fortune, in freedom, under our own sovereign rights and laws, to make our own decisions, as we have done for well over a thousand years, since our first Parliament in 1245.

Above all, I have sought to present a true portrait of the German aggressively self-centred mindset, unchanged through the ages, so aptly and unerringly described by their own cherished philosopher Nietzsche, within my text. I do not claim 100% accuracy, and originality, and have made grateful use of many recognised authorities and writers. We are all trying to convince and move our leaders in the right direction of true grasp and knowledge of the traps, laid so convincingly, by a series of some of the cleverest gamesters in this 'hooksters' paradise. Constructive criticism, correction, debate and argument are all welcome. At least it will indicate that my contribution has been read and marked. For the danger is both real and imminent to the Western world, and especially our beloved Britain. We band of Britain's true supporters and defenders from aggressive supranational dictatorship, must co-operate in support of our country's long-fought and hard-won freedom and sovereignty, to which I have devoted much of my life, and must continue to fight against the GEU efforts to reduce Britain to less than Third World status."

Harry Beckhough
Marlborough, June, 2008

Germany's First Reich

Nietzsche, German philosopher, said: "The German is an expert on secret paths to chaos." Churchill wrote: "The Germans, after all, had been belligerent for 2000 years. British public schoolboys were taught that Civilisation stops at the Rhine and the Danube. "A Hun alive is a War in prospect" (Biography William Manchester).

According to Gerald Flurry, the German roots go further back than Churchill's estimate of 2000 years of belligerency, right back to the Bible and Noah's son Shem. He bore a son Assur, progenitor of those fierce warriors, the Assyrians. Dr Hoch, in his *Compendium of World History* described ancient Assyria as "the greatest war-making power in history, dedicated to ferocity, bloodshed and manslaughter. Fabled for their fierce barbarism". "The Assyrians came down like a wolf on the fold." That same barbaric vein continued in their descendants, named by Tacitus c. 55 A.D. as: "The Germani, warlike people". So they ever have remained, warlike and ever aggressive, even in defeat. Evinced in Tiglath Pileser lst, Emperor of Assyria, who conquered Babylon c.1100 BC., hated and feared for his ruthlessness and cruelty in warfare.

James McCabe (*History of the World*) names the Assyrians: "a fierce, treacherous race - they never kept faith when it was in their interest to break treaties". Hitler, likewise, totally egoistic, broke faith, promises, treaties, contracts, agreements (as with the Russians, attacking them in 1941, without warning, despite his solid agreement with Stalin, who believed him implicitly), whenever it suited his selfish purpose. Unprovoked war, without warning, i.e. ruthless treachery, lies and deceit are all common in German history from the outset. Abraham, from Shem's third son Arphaxad, was the complete opposite, being peace-loving in his unique faith in One God.

Jerome, the historian, c 340 AD, wrote of Indo-Germanic tribes, including 'Assur', invading Europe. Ever fiercely ambitious, the Assyrians, about 800 BC, were prepared to take the whole world by storm. The collapse of the Assyrian Empire fuelled mass emigration, West and North, across the mainland of Europe. By the time of Tacitus (c 55 - 117 AD.) these warlike Germani had settled in there. By 476 AD. the Germanic Kingdoms brought down the Western half of the Roman Empire by fierce battles, and Alaise took Rome. The Carlingians took over in the

730s, and Pepin III was crowned in 751 as Christian King.

Charlemagne (Charles the Great 771-843), heir to Pepin, marched into Italy in 774 to protect the Pope, who was under attack from angry dissenters. In 799 he again rescued that same Pope Lee III, beaten and imprisoned by conspirators, enjoying his favour thereafter. In 800 Charlemagne was officially welcomed to Rome and crowned Emperor by the grateful Pope in St. Peters, on Christmas Day. Thus the old Roman imperial title was revived and conferred on Charlemagne.

He became, therefore, Founder and First Emperor of the Holy Roman Empire, and subjugated by *Blut und Stahl* (blood and steel), every German tribe to Roman Catholicism, except the hardy Saxons, who refused. He thus spread the Christian faith by violent, bloody means, forcing his brand of Christianity overall. Yet he was later worshipped as Leader of the Holy Roman Empire - though his bonds to the ancient Romans were far from holy.

Otto 1st, the Great (936 to 973 AD.) was a ruthless warrior, anointed King of Germany in Aachen. Pope John II appealed to him for protection, and he responded. The Pope then bestowed the imperial crown on Otto in 962. He, in turn, extended Christianity by brute force. For the following 800 years German kings called themselves "Roman Emperors of the German Nation". Thus the disparate German tribes were welded together, becoming the imperial race, with a growing feeling of national kinship.

In 1074, the Charter of Worms was issued, without episcopal intervention. Henry V (1106-1128) was a resourceful, but brutal, treacherous ruler, continuing the Germanic habit of breaking promises and agreements. He fought tough, brutal, killing wars against Hungary, Poland and Bohemia. He then fought through Italy to secure the imperial crown. Pope Paschal, humiliated, was forced to resign all secular holdings of the Church, except the See of Rome. Pope and Emperor were henceforth bitter rivals. The long struggle of Welf und Waiblinger (Hohenstaufen), ended in 1135, the Year of Pacification in Germany. Such peace in Germany obviously could not last, with such ever-warlike people, always fighting and feuding. Frederick 1st led the 3rd Crusade to enjoy more heavy fighting and mass killing in the name of Christendom.

Civil War broke out in Germany 1197 to 1212, inciting citizens to bloodlust and murder, causing utter chaos throughout the empire, with family strife and bloodshed. Then came the Great Interregnum in 1250, with a period of internal confusion and disorder, leaving Germany in a continuing state of family feuds, revenge killings, assassinations and general mayhem. All that had been so painstakingly pieced together from Charlemagne onward, aiming to make one great, consolidated German Empire, now being torn apart. The aggressive German people, without their necessary strong, imperial leader, now lost their way, resorting to petty, internecine struggles, feuds, fighting in family and gangs.

In 1438 Albert of Habsburg became Habsburg Emperor through to the dissolution of the Holy Roman Empire. But 1517 brought major change, when Martin Luther (miner's son become monk, become priest and then professor of theology at the University of Wittenberg), called for reform of the Roman Catholic Church. His Probes into functions of the Church spread rapidly throughout Germany. In 1517, Luther nailed to the Wittenberg Church door, 95 Theses against misuse of absolution and indulgences, followed in 1519 by Luther burning the papal Bull, for which he was excommunicated. The basic Lutheran doctrine was justification by faith alone, making priestly offices of the Catholics unnecessary, as intermediary between individual and God. 1543 Copernicus published Luther's *De Revolutionibus Orbium Coelestricum*, claiming the Papacy had no control over eternal mystery of death.

The Coronation of Charles V as Emperor at Bologna, was the last of a German emperor by the Pope. The Thirty Years War (1618-48), was fought between the Roman Catholic Emperor Charles and other Catholic princes and states, in a furious vicious contest against a network of Protestant towns and principalities. Germany was devastated, lost large parts of her population and her empire's borders were reduced and narrowed. However, at the Peace of Westphalia 1648, Germany's feudal princes gained full sovereignty. After the Thirty Years War, came the beginning of the Brandenburg-Prussia rise to pre-eminence amongst German states. In 1701 Frederick lst, Elector of Brandenburg, took the title of King of Prussia, crowning himself at Königsberg.

Frederick William I (1713-1740), son of Frederick I, established a formidable army, based on strict military training and discipline. He laid the foundation of the future power of Prussia, backed by a strong war machine, thoroughly trained for immediate, powerful action. Frederick II, (1740-86) of Prussia, expanded Prussian strength and military might, enlarging Prussian territories, making Prussia the second most powerful German kingdom after Austria. Famed for building a formidable army of military strength, discipline and ferocity.

Germany's Second Reich

The Napoleonic Wars brought the end of the Holy Roman Empire, 1806. The Congress of Vienna, 1814, saw the map of Europe and Germany redrawn. The 39 resultant German states were united within the German Confederation, dominated by Austria. But the Habsburg monarchy (1815-48), brought about the real unification of Germany. Pan-Germanism, produced Goethe and Nature, *Sturm und Drang* (exaltation of Germanism), Schiller and Beethoven, Lessing, Mozart, Bach and philosophy. 1790-1815: Followed by Romanticism and classic tradition until death of Goethe and Beethoven. Then followed, for a short spell, the eternal laws of Nature, in Germanic version, with country idylls.

Germany always considered herself ordained to be the greatest in Europe, supported by her philosophers: Hegel said: 'Germany had the right and duty to project her national image over all Europe. German philosophy was its direct expression'. Hegel appealed for the 'Strong Master who should mould the German masses.'

Fichte thought Germany was the Nation 'par excellence' – with the right to achieve the foundation of her nationhood by force, using further force and trickery to assure its hegemony, resorting to the craftiest deceit and presumption of 'rights'. Jahn, in 1809, declared Germany the Holy Race succeeding the Hebrews and the Hellenes.

Arnt, in 1803, said each State must fight the neighbour states, when they rob it of the air and light it needed for development: i.e. *Lebensraum. He suggested they partition Poland, and annexe Holland and Switzerland as 'natural conquests'.* Nietzsche said: 'Germany has always been and always will be: "of yesterday, of tomorrow, but never of today".

Heine's clear prophecy of 1834, that *'the Germans were returning to a past, that might well inspire them one day, to the most violent, political revolution the Continent had ever known'.* A true vision!

William I (1838-1880) accomplished the merger of Prussia with Germany He established his own version of a trained, disciplined Army. Count Otto von Bismarck became Prime Minister in 1862, as also Foreign

Minister of Prussia. Supported strongly by Wilhelm 1, he used his own sound, effective diplomatic skills in gaining general acceptance of Germany. In 1866 the Prussian Army crushed Austria in 7 weeks. Prussia then annexed most of the remaining North German states and, with 17 smaller German states, formed a federal union, called the *North German Confederation,* to make a united German nation, the German Empire, of which William I of Prussia, was proclaimed Emperor. By early 20th century, Germany had become Europe's leading industrial nation. A remarkable, strategic relationship was growing between Germany and Russia, due to the diplomatic skill of Bismarck. Looking far ahead, he could see the future benefits of a strong compact with Russia, securing each other's borders.

The problems of the Balkan Peninsula temporarily interfered with this firm relationship. But in 1881 Bismarck resurrected the Alliance, nursing it carefully until its break-up again in 1887, forced him temporarily out of office. However, he remained determined to extend the German Empire, always a first German priority, since their beginning. Bismarck ruled as Head of dynasty until 1890, when Wilhelm II sacked him over disagreement on policy with Russia. Instead Russia formed a new and lasting alliance with France, firmly resurrected after WWII, using France as intermediary and agent.

Archduke Ferdinand of Austria (1889-1914) was assassinated 28th June 1914, on a State visit to Sarajevo, by Bosnian revolutionaries. Using this as a thin excuse, on 1st August 1914, the ill-starred Kaiser Wilhelm II, physically and mentally unbalanced, plunged the world into the bloodiest war ever perpetrated by the aggressive Germans. World War I, started by a deranged egocentric, seeking his own vain glory, set in motion the most stupid, unwarranted, bloodiest years of outright murder of over 18 million, mainly young men, most in their teens, with some 20 million wounded, plus prisoners of war, leaving behind millions of suffering, broken families. The abject figure of yet another German leader, seeking ambitiously to rule the world, but again ending in chaos and world hatred, fled ignominiously to exile in Holland.

Most people thought the Germans would, at long last, have learnt their goriest lesson, to cease such madness. But, as Churchill said, "They never change". They seem convinced that their destiny is to rule the world, and they never cease working towards that end, no matter what the cost. They continue to cheat, lie and deceive their trusting neighbours, pretending friendship and co-operation, whilst pursuing their demonic schemes. Linked always with the Russians, from whom they learnt and assimilated the Leninist skills of continuous lies and deceit.

Nietzsche, their discerning philosopher, declared: "It is not for nothing they are called the *Täusche Volk* (the deceitful people). The German soul has its passageways and inter-passageways; there are caves, hideouts and dungeons in it; its disorder has a good deal of attraction of the mysterious; the German is an expert on secret paths to chaos. The German loves clouds and everything that is unclear, becoming twilit, damp and overcast; whatever is in anyway uncertain, unformed, blurred, growing, he feels to be profound" – viz: the development of the European Union, adopted by Germany as cover for her plans to control Europe.

At the Treaty of Versailles, Article 231, Germany accepted sole responsibility for starting the War. Germany, ever-aggressive, caused the death of some 18 million people overall in this stupid, unnecessary war, costing so many valuable young lives, with some 20 million wounded, in the senseless, ill-led years of trench slaughter in the killing fields of France. The Allies said they would control and suppress Germany's military growth and power, to prevent future aggression. But, only 21 years later, Hitler brought about another unwarranted, self-created, killing World War. His demonic vision creating even greater aggression, causing the death of some 50 million people, with millions wounded and 192,000 live prisoners – many killed regardless.
Proving once again that they NEVER learn from the hard lessons of defeat, never change for the better, never repent of their evil ways and never improve. They remain totally deceitful, aggressive and untrustworthy, false masters of lies and deceit, as history decisively reveals. They still succeed in deceiving most of our ever-trusting Western world, as well as large parts of the East, *especially with their criminal activities in the Balkans* – yet able to steer the West, especially their main target America, into believing they were behaving properly, and presenting an acceptable case for the use of American arms in their support. How easily we seem, in the West, to be hooked by these skilful, deceptive game-players.

Another perfect example of deceit, was the way the Germans outmanoeuvred, cunningly, the terms of the Versailles Treaty. It forbade

Germany possession or construction of any large guns. No military aircraft, no submarines, no warships; limitation on the size of the German Army, with no conscripts permitted. But, aggressive, cunning and deceitful as ever, Germany immediately began plotting and planning ways around such firm conditions, so as to prepare, in advance, for the next war. The great strength of the Prussian-built German Army was its General Staff. They were left in place, untouched, by the Allies, too busy with their own immediate foolish reductions of men and armaments, thinking Germany finally and completely crushed and beaten: Well before the advent of Hitler, the German General Staff were preparing for the next war, with full complement of officers, fully trained.

As early as 1922, German Army leaders made a secret deal with the Russian Red Army to assemble weapons in Russian plants, in exchange for major loans and training of Russian troops. Construction progressed apace, until Germany became bold enough to build new ships, from passenger liners to warships, and arms in homeland factories, defiantly and openly. No adverse reaction from disarmed Europe or America emboldened the Germans to break all Versailles controls, typically, again bold and arrogant, defying any interference, knowing the West too weak and self-centred to bother. Germany, was secretly preparing for the next war.

Politically, after the failure of the unpopular Weimar Republic, with upsurge in unemployment and the collapse of markets and currency, trouble was brewing, especially the lack of leadership, causing great unrest. In 1925, the aged Field Marshal Hindenburg, was elected President, hoping his image as War Leader, would pacify. But the Great Depression began before 1929 with massive unemployment and inflation, and grew ever worse, failing leadership in every respect.

Germany's Third Reich

Hitler's National Socialist Party emerged in 1930, in their military style uniforms, gaining popular support and 107 seats at Election. The collapse of Weimar Government, Hindenburg ill and out of action, left the way open for the American/German Banks, financiers and other Powers supporting Hitler to pressure the dying Hindenburg to replace his own first choice, of experienced Statesman von Papen, as his successor, with Adolf Hitler's guaranteed restoration of order. In 1933 Hitler assumed power, making his first oratorical, impassioned speeches, which I heard whilst on Student Course at Freiburg. Quickly forcing his Enablement Bill through the Reichstag, he declared himself "President of the German Third Reich" to general acclaim, with full martial panoply and theatrical display. Now with full dictatorial power, he dismissed all other Parties and closed down all Trade Unions, becoming Supremo! (Now being copied by the Constitution/Treaty of the European Union under German Command to full dictatorship).

So, fatefully, this uneducated, untaught, long unemployed ex-decorator, Austrian born Schickelgruber, one-time Corporal in the German Army, ex-convict, became, by strange twist of Fate, Chancellor of Germany. Events followed quickly. The wilful burning of the Reichstag, Berlin, the Law of Nuremberg which followed in 1935, depriving Jews of the rights of citizenship – as first step along the devilish road to their monstrous total annihilation – some 6 million of God's creatures, men, women and children.

Along with them went gypsies, disabled, coloureds and others who disputed his leadership. No mercy, no compunction, just wholesale slaughter, whether by shooting, burning or poison gas – after fiendish, medical and surgical experiments for mind control. How to measure the emotions, or mental stability, of the thousands of Germans who carried out these maniacal slaughters of fellow human beings? It is not simply that they automatically obey the orders of superiors, but that they could actually bring themselves to such cold-blooded murder of large numbers of innocent people, including babies. They neither answer nor conform to any normal criterion. Hitler's demonic leadership grew ever more dynamic and emotionally wildly demanding, as his mental state of instability worsened – so that he even slaughtered his own faithful followers,

Roehm and his Brownshirts, in that notorious 'Night of the long knives' – thinking they were acting treasonably. His bullying Nazi followers, in their military-style uniforms and jack boots, beat up all resistance, smashing all Jewish-owned shop windows in one impassioned effort called "Crystalnacht". They burnt disallowed Jewish and other authors' books and music in every town market place, robbing the owners and sending them off to death in concentration camps.

The world once again turned its face away, to its everlasting shame, pretending it would all soon just go away. Of course it did not, for beneath this bloodthirsty surface, much deeper plots were being developed. The continuous theme of German expansion *(Lebensraum),* the surrounding areas and lands to annexe, before developing that ever-sought conquest of all Europe. Piece by piece they work on subverting each area, East and West.

Just one lone voice, that of the intrepid, far-seeing, most experienced Parliamentarian, Winston Churchill, rose to warn Britain and the world. He was continuously well-informed from knowledgeable sources, including some hidden German opposition to Hitler. Not only was no notice taken of him and his dire warning but, in that era of appeasement, he was mocked and vilified by Press, media and Parliament. In addition, his appointments, positions and offices were removed by Chamberlain, PM, sending him to the Back Benches in Parliament – but they could not silence him. The world owes its post-war freedom to that stubborn, canny, far-seeing patriot, whose inborn love of Country and people overrode all problems of military strength, political or religious faiths (he had an American Jewish mother), party and group divides. Would that we had him now to defend us from the new German onslaught! And point clearly the truth hidden within the deceits of the (German European Union (GEU).

Eventually, the bitter realisation of the failure of all Chamberlain's shameful, weak appeasement attempts made Parliament rise, as one man, to demand Churchill as Prime Minister and Leader in War, to defend and save the United Kingdom. Unfortunately in 1919 Britain disarmed, becoming ill-equipped and unprepared to fight any war. Despite Churchill's warnings and pleadings, disarmament had been carved out to great extent in all Services since the Versailles Treaty, leaving Britain well-nigh defenceless against any major attack. Every Ministry of Defence seems imbued with the same madness, our present situation continuing this lack of support, so necessary to maintain our Armed Forces in full strength, to remain equal to the every-widening tasks imposed on them globally, with the world-wide menace of terrorism, leaving us uncovered.

That same idiocy of all-round disarmament still continues, after our lack of preparedness almost caused defeat in WWII, with all the dire consequences. Even now, our brave troops of all services, but especially the Army, are sent into battle desperately short of the arms and equipment so necessary for their personal protection, as well as ability to overcome the enemy – and meet global demands on our military and peace defensive ability, so highly respected worldwide. A role the EU cannot match in its desire to take the place of NATO.

With terrorist threats already casting a forward shadow of the possibility of WWIII, we simply cannot afford to neglect our Armed Forces, to whom we need now add a highly trained armed division of our Police Force. The evil of terrorism recognises no boundaries – nor any respect for human life. We need to rethink our strategies and widen the vastly important role of trained expert Intelligence Services to uncover all evil schemes, before they reach realisation. We are now operating in a different world, where brother cannot trust brother, let alone nations trust contracts for common defence.

We have lost the keen edge, which held our defences, and brought us final victory. Britain is at her best when defending her own country and people. But no country can continue to stand alone as we did in 1940/41. We need trustworthy allies, as our Commonwealth and American cousins have proven, in those German world-wars of 1914 and 1939. We are suffering extreme debilitation, tied to the taskmasters of Europe. Let us regain our historic true freedom, and the ability to choose trustworthy allies in America and our own Commonwealth, to root out these evil terrorists, and once more stand guardian to the peaceful existence of our own country and the rest of the world.

Hitler wrote *Mein Kampf* in prison. He had visions of himself as the German Messiah, with a mandate to lead his people to conquer Europe, possibly the whole world. Benito Mussolini named his régime "The Holy Roman Empire." Hitler also saw his Third Reich as the "Holy Roman Empire." Both régimes were born of the devil. Hitler said "We are not a movement, rather we are a religion – I'm going to become a religious figure." He was motivated by worship of an extreme cult. Above all, from a misconception of the Jesuit order. His élite SS wore the devil's sacred *Hakenkreuz* (swastika – crooked cross) with black uniforms, as his

"Society of Jesus". A love/hate crazed relationship, for he descended to paganism.

Hitler's impassioned, wild, aggressive, heavy oratory moved the German people often to match his hysteria, with military music and impressive stage-setting, with massed rows of marching, uniform-clad youth. His *Deutsche Volk* responded eagerly, arms uplifted to this new hero, who promised them work and a full stomach. Exceptions, had to keep themselves well hidden. If discovered, they received short shrift from teams of assassins. The Vatican besought God's blessing on the Reich, with Church and State co-operating. German bishops were ordered to swear allegiance to the Nazi regime. Hitler actually believed that the Germans were God's chosen people, selected for aggressive expansion to rule over all people – quite manic. But the Nazis turned to paganism and Wagner with false images of imagined heroism.

In 1935 a Plebiscite in the Saar Basin brought reunion with Germany. Then, in 1936, Germany reoccupied the Rhineland – There followed the Berlin-Rome Axis with Franco of Spain, and a German-Japanese Pact. Hitler, now emboldened at lack of response from the Allies, ventured further, invading Austria in 1938, with the annexation of Sudetenland, adding some 6 million Germans to his increasing roll of Germans regained, and fully supportive. The Ribbentrop-Molotov non-aggression pact, August 1939, secured Germany's Eastern flank. March 1939 marked his bold move for *Lebensraum* with the annexation of Czecho-Slovakia, pleading 'Sudetenland' as German, and claiming he was supporting their rights. Whilst the World held its breath and the British, with Churchill, were calling for immediate action to stop this growing wilful aggression, weak Chamberlain reneged on Britain's Czech ally, shaming Britain by declaring it: "A far-off country of no significance." Hitler made best use of Chamberlain's weak 'appeasement' tactics. Anthony Eden, Foreign Secretary, resigned in protest against such shameful appeasement. By now the Germans had succeeded in arousing in their neighbours the terror of which they were expert, deliberately promoted by Karl von Clausewitz as Schrecklichkeit (terror), the Prussians strategist's secret weapon to shorten wars. In the 1914 War German troops behaved 'frightfully', executing without mercy civilians, hostages, prisoners, as ordered by superiors. Barbara Tuchman wrote: "Suddenly the world became aware of the beast beneath the German skin".

Hitler now believed he could attack Poland, with full strength, with massive brutal bombing into defeat – it was the most merciless massacre against a well-nigh helpless adversary, desperately fighting to the last, whilst Russia looked on! But this was Hitler's move too far. At last Chamberlain, forced into action, had to honour the pledge to Poland by Britain and France. He now warned Hitler personally, but defiant Hitler believed Britain would again abstain. So he declared war on Poland on 3rd September 1939. On that same day Britain and France, perforce, declared War on Germany. After crushing Poland in open massacre, Hitler's appetite was now whetted for Europe, with his master-plan all carefully prepared by his modernised Services.

The German war machine, at full strength, with a huge army array of the most modern, fully equipped tanks, fighter aircraft, warships and submarines, now let loose an all-powerful *Blitzkrieg*, smashing their way, at top speed, across Europe, sweeping all before their carefully rehearsed advance, led by the most professional German General Staff, trained by Prussian military might, creating fear and *Schrecklichkeit* (terror) everywhere. Terror was their watchword, brutal and merciless. Europe's poor defences crumbled, the 'immovable' Maginot line smashed asunder, France (with a bigger army) caved in, and Hitler marched, in swaggering triumph, down the Champs Elysées of Paris. The British Forces, betrayed by the Belgian/French collapse, without warning, did well to escape in part at Dunkirk, aided by a host of English ships and small boats, rescuing them courageously off the beaches, despite heavy gunfire.

Britain, now left alone, with brave Churchill, a lone figure, courageously defying the Nazi-German armoured might. Under his fearless guidance, the United Kingdom, did unite with strong will, to produce the lacking military, and train volunteers eager to join the Services, but still lacking weapons. I was trained at Catterick and Larkhill in 1940 as a 'theoretical' Royal Artillery officer, never having fired a gun – but we learnt under good instruction. Within weeks the whole country was on war footing, with Commonwealth countries and Allies joining in. No heroics, just grim determination by an unready country, lacking guns, modern weapons, almost any weapons, save those remaining from WWI. The British people strove day and night continuously to build the planes, guns, shells, all the urgently needed armaments and weapons of war, so badly neglected by our 'comfortable' leaders. That was true heroism, with our women doing a man's job, helping literally in defence and attack. But our Ministry of Defence never seems to learn.

In 1940 Germany attacked Britain, principally at first by air. Heavily outnumbered, the British pilots fought day and night, beating off and shooting down the German planes, which outnumbered the British by at least 3 to 1. Failing with their fighter attacks, Goering then ordered Luftwaffe heavy bombers to attack British cities, principally London, breaking the established rules of War. London, especially, was pounded day and night, as also other major cities, continuously, to a mass of rubble and smashed buildings, in flames. Many thousands of lives were lost and bodies broken, with frightful damage – until they were finally beaten off and withdrew. The British people remained defiant throughout. This was German War, slaughtering huge numbers of unarmed women and children, expecting to terrify them into surrender. Then shrieking with horror when the RAF retaliated.

Hitler's main plan was to invade a beaten Britain – as promised by Goering with his vastly superior Luftwaffe force, by Spring 1941 – in good time to spring his second trap – the unbelievable invasion of Russia. But Hitler's plans were going awry. Britain should have been invaded and conquered, reduced to abject surrender by Spring 1941. Instead, those stubborn British had beaten off Goering's invasion fleet, and forced delays to Hitler's plan, so that the Russian operation had to begin in late summer. Moscow and other cities put up determined resistance and inevitably came the icy Russian winter. Downpours of snow and ice clogging the roads began to hold up tanks, guns and heavy armour. The *Blitzkrieg* ground to a halt and troops were frozen in their tracks. The invasion turned to defeat and rout. The great German Army began to retreat – against Hitler's orders, and it now became a race against time to reach Germany, in time to stop the threatening Russian invasion. It was a costly defeat, fulfilling Nietzsche's prophecy of ending in chaos.

Meanwhile the RAF, now better equipped, began to repay the Luftwaffe's merciless coverage bombing of major cities, especially London, with merited interest. British Intelligence, Station X, based at Bletchley Park, broke German top ciphers of 'unbreakable' Enigma, and 'Lorenz', enabling German warships and submarines to be exactly pin-pointed, traced and sunk by British Navy. The Luftwaffe, similarly pin-pointed by Bletchley Code-breakers, withdrew, beaten! America entered the European War as Britain's major Ally, after the Japanese treacherous attacks on the U.S. Navy at Pearl Harbor, without warning, December 1941. Before end of 1942, Rommel's Africa Corps were heavily defeated in the Desert Campaign at el Alamein by the British 8th Army (in which we Codebreakers played our part), and chased into Italy, where they suffered further defeats by British and American forces, finally withdrawing their remnants back to Germany. Meanwhile the Americans were attacking and defeating the Japanese forces in the Pacific, heading for Japan whilst the British 14th Army was attacking the Japanese, who had invaded Burma – with my Group breaking Japanese signals, for competent General Bill Slim.

In June 1944, the Allies mounted a carefully-planned invasion of German-dominated France, over Normandy beaches. The Germans were put to flight in Europe, the Allies clearing Holland, Belgium and moving across France, despite heavy resistance, to enter Paris to great acclaim, free again of German occupation. The Germans, pursued back into their homeland, for the first time in their history, both West from the Allies and East from Russia, were totally defeated, with many of their cities, including Berlin, in ruins. Chaos reigned again in Germany. Hitler committed suicide in his Berlin bunker, May 1945. I saw his body under tarpaulin, outside his bunker, as *memento mori*.

The Nazis were totally defeated and disgraced, but not finally finished. From the end of 1943, through to 1945, a great many leaders, scenting defeat, had escaped from Germany, some to Switzerland but many, using Vatican 'rat-lines', were helped escape to Spain, Portugal – even across U.S.A. to South America and Mexico, Columbia and Argentina, taking huge quantities of stolen treasure from their victims. They bought industrial companies to gain power-base in each country. They had huge caches in Swiss banks and Liechtenstein. They set up an International office in Madrid and kept in touch with Chancellor Konrad Adenauer, who confessed to me that he had taken back 134 ex-Nazis, now working with his staff in Bonn (cf John Loftus *Unholy Trinity,*1991).

Germany's Fourth Reich – The New Beginning

So it continues: after each defeat, they are already preparing for the next aggression. Their nature never changes, as has been stated by Churchill, Nietzsche and others, as is now, once again, clearly apparent. Those who scuttled, opened new international offices in Madrid, planning a new approach to their commitment to conquer Europe. This time, after so many repeated military defeats (especially from the stubborn British and American Allies), they sought a different tack, first by economic means, with the provided EU set-up ready to hand, to be taken over and used for their purpose. Under the cloak of European Union they could weave new plans for domination of all Europe.

In 1941 Walter Funk, Hitler's economics Minister, launched *Europäische Wirtschafts-gemeinschaft* (European Economic Community) – to establish a single European currency, the Reichsmark. Plus the integration of all European economies into a "Single Market". The creation of a Common Agricultural Policy (CAP) was based on the mode of European agriculture, protected by subsidies and high tariffs, keeping prices artificially high for the benefit, principally, of French and German small farmers. This Franco-German benefit was later enshrined, post-war, under Article 39 of the Treaty of Rome. Similar to the later Maastricht Treaty of EU, with a PanEuropean Bank (Bank Europa) created and run by Germany, in Frankfurt.

This, then, was the embryo Nazi plan for the future of greater Europe, all combined under the sole command of the master, 'Aryan' superior German Superstate, cum dictatorship. Yet, after the most decisive defeat in all their history, still in existence in primary positions, a considerable number of the perpetrators of these evil plans – after ruthlessly murdering millions who appeared to be obstacles to their greater glory. The very name of Concentration Camps brings the vision of the devil who possesses their souls. So that same inbuilt German habit of lying deceit continued during, and after WWII, in even more cunning, false operations, at which they are past-masters, as if schooled by Lenin, world master of lies and corruption.

Thus, Arthur Spiegelman reported: "Realising they were losing the War in 1944, Nazi leaders met major German industrialists to plan a secret, post-war network to restore them to power" (extract from a newly classified U.S. document). Krupp and others were told to be prepared to finance the *Underground Nazi Continuance Party* to create a future, strong German Empire. "Over 500 million dollars were transferred out of Germany – to lay the foundation for future re-emergence." This document was concealed from the American and British people. The U.S. Intelligence Agencies made the deadly error of inaction instead of immediate exposure of the truth to kill off these Nazi carefully prepared forward plans, already activated. What reason could they have had – a mistrust of their own people? Or connivance from above with aid of CFR? Whilst the Allies were planning to preserve the peace of the world, the Germans were already contriving to win the Battle of the Peace. They never desist in their aggressive attempt to dominate first Europe, and then the World.

Incredibly, Ernest Bevin, British Minister, convinced by the astute Germans, as were the American Statesmen, that Communism was the greatest post-war threat in Germany, transferred all British Intelligence operations (still concentrating on anti-Nazi measures), to hunt the few remaining, weak Communist cells from 1947 onwards. Ex-Nazis were still in profusion. Communists there were practically none. So Bevin, fooled by the Germans, transferred all efforts to total search for Communists in 1947 and, unbelievably, told the Germans to *denazify themselves*. He should have heard the Germans laugh at 'British stupidity'!

Dr. Konrad Adenauer, known as 'the old fox' for his total deceit of America, (thus producing large quantities of dollars), boasted his ability to hoodwink the Americans. Far from chasing Communists, he was on friendly terms with Russia. *General Karl Haushofer (from Ribbentrop's Treasury), was convinced that Germany, and Russia could combine to control the whole world.* Adenauer's Government was riddled with ex-Nazis. Drs. Hans Globke and Herbert Blankenborn, Government leaders, served the Nazis, drafting Hitler's race-laws and the Holocaust. Globke was charged by Dr. Lütkens with packing the Foreign Office with 94 ex-Nazis from Ribbentrop's office. Friend of Reinhard Gehlen whose network of spies were an arm of the Bonn Government. Adenauer admitted that two thirds of his top diplomats were ex-Nazis, claiming he could not build his Foreign Office without their skills. Dr. Theodor Overlander, Minister for Expellees, was responsible for the murder of Polish Jews. He ordered the SS to wipe out Lvov city completely.

In 1950 the *Nazi Madrid Circular* (intercepted by British Intelligence), to satellite centres Bonn, Lisbon, Buenos Aires etc., said:
"Germany has always considered orientation towards the West, as a policy of expedience. All of our national leaders have constantly counselled the long-range policy of close co-operation with the EAST. *The so-called American democracy does not deserve the bones of a single German soldier. What Germany needs in the future is not democracy, but a system of statecraft, similar to that of the Soviet dictatorship. Enabling the political and military elite in Germany to organise the industrial capacity of Europe, and the military qualities of the German people, for the revival of the German race and the re-establishment of Europe as power-centre of the world. We will surely gain the undisputed leadership in Europe, NOT excluding Britain.*

Madrid was the Nazi International Geopolitical Control Centre. *Die Spinne* was the Nazi organisation in Spain, Portugal, Morocco, Sweden, Argentina, Buenos Aires etc. All now followed General Haushofer's Plan. "German orientation towards the East! The new shape of German aggression!" Other units were named *Edelweiss, Konsul, Scharnhorst, Odessa* (of the Nazi élite Guard) – *all promoting resurgence to a German Europe.* In 1945 the German Master-plan (captured by the Allies) included a European Peace order (like Adenauer's), a European Union on Federal basis, a Commonwealth between Germany, Bohemia and Moravia, and an economic integration of Europe.

In February 1945 Churchill and Roosevelt signed a document: "It is our inflexible purpose to destroy German militarism and Nazism, and to ensure Germany will NEVER again be able to disrupt and disturb the peace of the world. We are determined to disarm and disband German Armed Forces and break up the German General Staff, that has contributed repeatedly to the resurgence of German militarism."

Little did they know of the plans well-in-hand BEFORE War-end, of German resuscitation. Krupp and Thyssen, the uncrowned Kings of Essen, were quickly and secretly rebuilt, with arranged co-operation abroad. Other industries had planned with the Nazi leaders (who went underground well before War-end), to set aside secure means of a speedy reconstitution for aggressive domination of Europe, now by political and economic means. Adenauer wrote: "National Socialism could not have come to power in Germany, if it had not found, in broad strategy of the population, soil prepared for its sowing of poison". That same illusion of being the master race, destined to dominate and rule over Europe, if not the world, passed down as their inheritance from the Assyrians, was still, as ever, their abiding belief. But now they had, at last, learnt the valuable lesson that they could not so succeed by force of arms alone.

Re-learning Lenin's philosophy of 'gain and succeed by deceit' they now threw their strength behind the creation of the EU in its new form. This became an illusion, winning over all nations, step by step. Developed from the Monnet/Schuman Plan, with Germany working cunningly and tirelessly behind the scenes, moving the pieces at will, to shape the stages of the *ephemeral GEU, Europe's greatest ever House of Cards.* Their Master-plan came from Friedrich Johann Strauss, Premier of Bavaria, Leader of Christian Socialist Group, who said: "We must find a new Starting Point which changes the face of the world" Strauss realised the inevitable crushing defeat into chaos of another World War. So he advised the way back by subtler, craftier means, with contrite seeming pretence of seeking only to make good by peace- making efforts as an unassuming member of a European federation. Strauss said "Our European attitude was the only escape hatch approach to make a come-back possible". He set his grand design for Germany's future mastery of Europe (to be faithfully followed by future leaders), with 10 key objectives:

1 - Destroy the legend that Germany is a country congenitally devoted to aggression — by Europeanisation of the German question, using Europe as cover.

2 - Persuade the Soviet Union into radically changing its policy towards Europe and Germany.

3 - Persuade Europe to become a Federation, sacrificing national pride and sovereignty.

4 - Europe must expand its own potential from the Atlantic to the Urals.

5 - Europe to include Poland, Czechoslovakia, Hungary and other Eastern countries.

6 - To counter fragmentation of the European continent, and ensure peace, separate national thinking in West and East Europe must be abandoned.

7 - Germany's specific territorial aims: a strong United States of Europe constructed with freedom of movement for every citizen, and free choice where to work and live....(all carefully prepared for the future Constitution).

8 - Unification of East with West Germany, to be seen as part of a general settlement uniting Germany.

9 - West European states to become members of a European defence community, with its own atomic armaments. (Which would be extremely dangerous for Europe and the world! Imagine just one atomic bomb on London).

10 - Germany must accept the long way round, patiently achieving step by step, harmonisation with Russia, America and East and West. Also achieve reform of NATO or replacement.

All Strauss's objectives have been fulfilled progressively as long-term basis of the German planned EU Constitution, under German dominant control. No contrition, no retribution, no sympathy. They remain totally deceitful, untrustworthy, masters of lies and pretence, as history decisively reveals, with our ever-trusting West and much of the East succumbing to their 'spin'. Despite their criminal activities in the Balkans, persuading the West, repeatedly fooled, into partaking in their cunning plots. Arranging German Plants and factories to be designed for possible quick conversion to war production, thus preparing in advance for the next aggression.

In the meantime, the Marshall European Recovery Plan 1947, born of America's foremost fear of Communism, brought closer economic co-operation between European countries, to the immediate benefit of Germany. The 16 participating countries set up OEEC (Organisation for European Economic Co-operation), to administer the Plan successfully. It was a minor miracle of rehabilitation, Black Market ceased overnight, as we introduced the new German DeutschMark to restore Germany's currency to real value. No more barter of cigarettes and coffee. Remarkable speedy return of restored vigour to German industry. Strange that the Mark they loved all these years was given new life by us, creating the new DMark, which the German people still prefer to the euro.

NATO was created between America, Britain and European nations, because of the Cold War aftermath with Russia, In 1946 the European Union of Federalists brought together groups in European countries of Britain, Belgium, France, Italy, Netherlands, Luxembourg and Switzerland. The cause of European unity included powerful names like Leon Blum of France, Alcide de Gasperi, P.M. of Italy, and Belgian socialist Paul-Henri Spaak. Churchill lent his support saying: *"We are with Europe, but not of it. We are linked, but not compromised. We are interested and associated but NOT absorbed"*. Churchill never changed his position of assisting, but not joining as a member. His great, far-seeing wisdom should always have remained our guide, with his firm, never deviating policy for Britain: "For we dwell among our own people". Churchill was so wise (unlike most of his more easily hooked successors from Macmillan/Heath onward), not to be caught up in the eternal problems (especially accounts and budgets) and machinations of European Union states, led by Franco-Germany, using Britain as a major pawn.

The prime mover at that time was Jean Monnet, an Alsace cognac salesman, who gained his part-education travelling the world's international markets. He believed strongly in the total unity of European states, adapting the Loucheur-Mayrich earliest functionalist model of 1925, followed by the 1926 International Steel Agreement, an earlier model (forerunner of ECSC) set up after WWI. They seem to have cast the original mould, from which eventually developed into the EU. The Schuman Plan of 1950 for the 'European Coal and Steel Community' was eventually agreed between Germany and France. The 3 Benelux countries and Italy joined the Plan. But the British Prime Minister, Labour's Clement Attlee, rejected it point blank, saying:

"It was impossible for Britain to accept the principle, that, *the most economic forces of this country should be handed over to an authority that is utterly undemocratic and is responsible to nobody."*... Wise words from a Labour PM, which with Churchill's clear statement, should have guided our Statesmen ever after.

The Plot Continues

The Treaty of Rome (1957) was carefully constructed on functional lines, for future transmission to a supernational authority. First cunningly known as the 'Common Market' acceptable to all, believing it to be a straight forward trading agreement. The Nazis used the rhetoric of "European Unity", but did not reveal their planned intent of final union into one supreme authority of federal states'. They also raised propaganda to a new level, deceiving their own people, those they occupied and the rest of the world. They continue to be well-practised past-masters of the evil arts of lies and deceit, even outdoing the Leninists, with their dialectic deceit.

So real birth of EU was post WWI, as we have seen, but made little progress in the difficult after-war years of the 1920s and 1930s. Europe was suffering from its manifold hurts and problems, and post WWI life bore many predicaments for a multitude of families. Statesmen were fully absorbed in each country's affairs in the struggle to make both ends meet, after such a terrible conflict of phenomenal costs.

1946 was an even worse year of reckoning and grief, after WWII. France, torn apart in WWI, again in 1940 and fought over again from mid 1944, faced huge political, economic and, even worse, physical, as well as industrial reconstruction. At the same time, caught up in prolonged, violent colonial wars, Belgium and Portugal likewise. Austria, depressed under grim Soviet occupation, seeking to maintain a semblance of independence. Both Greece and Italy embroiled in civil wars.

Britain, heroic winner of the worst and most deadly combat in history, faced the repeated, ruinous massive costs and debts of prolonged war. Now, even worse for its proud history (reaching its peak of Empire in the 19th century), faced with the loss of its beloved colonies and her garnered wealth, at its peak, in the proud Victorian reign, at the turn of the century. Now, as a result of two unsought, terrible wars, losing the cream of its young, virile manhood, reduced to massive debts, with rising unemployment and the return of P.O.Ws, many severely injured.

Gone the splendid days of the Raj, when Britain proudly held her great Empire with surprisingly few officers and men. In the space of some 30 years and two world wars only 21 years apart, its century of glorious achievements torn asunder by that murderous, ever-aggressive state of Germany, uncontrollable even by its own imperfect leaders. Germany should have been broken up after WWI, then reduced to the collection of smaller states of its early years, and left to fight and murder amongst themselves.

Now the greater question: what to do to restore Europe? Churchill gave the best guidance: *"Help, by all means, but stay apart"*. Only that way, by holding on to our hard-won sovereignty will we be able to continue to be an independent nation, with our own laws and Parliament, and our own way of living, trading, keeping firm hold of all we have produced that is basically good. We still have our Commonwealth who stood loyally by us. We have our proven friend and Ally of America. By keeping our independence, we may best forge our future, and maintain good relations with Europe (who would be under the dictator's heel but for us and America – how easily they forget and how little gratitude!). That should be signal enough for us to take back our independence, which so many of our successive governments have bartered, or gambled away, without due thought of the wise guidance of Churchill. Time we woke up from this nightmare take-over, and realised we are once again under attack from Germany (now with intemperate France as Ally), before it is too late, and we discover that we have thrown away our ancient rights and independence – and gained dross.

To return to our post-war state: America, with her vast industry, became our major supplier throughout and, through helping us to final victory, emerged as the overall winner economically, industrially and financially. Europe owes her a debt of gratitude for the Marshall Plan, and other aid. As also the tremendous help we gave for years, at high cost, to help their resuscitation, though ourselves in dire straits, taking many years to recover, independent as ever, we fought our way back to a fairly healthy state generally.

Unfortunately, Germany finds it impossible to co-operate peacefully and honestly in Europe and Asia, without again embarking on her usual network of schemes for power in every area, employing her well-honed instruments of deceit and doubletalk, convincing NATO that her participation was necessary in the Western Army in 1950. So persuasive, that she actually won back her sovereign status and full membership of NATO by 1955 – a reward for her cunning dexterity, having been shut out postwar. All seem to succumb to Germany's suggestive manipulation, weaving schemes without real substance in Lenin style and Goebbels propaganda, German master of lies and connivance.

By clever manoeuvring Germany manipulated return of the Saar in 1957, as the 10th State of the Federal Republic. The Bundeswehr was recruited directly from the upper echelons of Hitler's Army, including Third Reich veteran Generals (cf Martin Lee: *The Beast Awakens,* 1997).

Expanding by Ratchets

In 1970 the renewed German-Soviet Treaty for "Friendship and co-operation" was signed, assuring their everlasting understanding – always included in Germany's secret plans for future control of greater Europe, both West and East – the same target as ever. It is truly amazing, on looking back, the ease with which Germany was able to deceive and convince America and Britain's leading Statesmen – as did Gorbachëv with his astute convincing stream of lies about his new Russia. Their joint ratchet found easy targets in the ever-trusting West.

East Germans overthrew their Communist regime in 1989, becoming one Germany in 1990/91. The German Democratic Republic became founder member of the Warsaw Treaty Organisation, by the Warsaw Pact with Russia, then occupying the Russian Zone of Germany. The Berlin Wall, built 1961, sealed off this Russian Zone from the West. In 1991 came the overthrow of the Soviet government. Yeltsin and Gorbachëv took power, expertly deceiving the West of their 'democratic' intentions.

In 1989 the Berlin Wall fell, bringing a neo-Nazi revival, cultivated strongly through the German Army (Bundeswehr), as the communist stranglehold on East Germany and Eastern Europe was relaxed. Violent racist incidents increased year on year to 1993, when the Bundestag passed an asylum law, setting firm restrictions on immigrants seeking asylum, further reports of neo-Nazi revival in Germany. In June 1991 the Bundestag moved their Capital back to Berlin from Bonn (Adenauer's home town). The fall of the Berlin Wall brought visible signs of return of the old spirit of independent arrogance. Now, a bona fide world power, second only to the U.S. in arms exports, with a standing army of circa 350,000, the largest in Europe. Already leading the EU and hoping soon to become a major nuclear power: Back on top by deceitful clever manoeuvring.

In 1990 a secret agreement between Gobachëv and Chancellor Kohl transferred the Bohemian and Moravian region to the Germans: Also the final division of Czechoslovakia and Yugoslavia by end of 1992. Germany planned to make a Customs Union of Europe, like Bismarck. Warnings by Roger Eatwell's: *Fascism*, Bernard Connolly's: *The Rotten Heart of Europe* and Margaret Thatcher's: *The Downing Street Years* – all go unheeded in our sleepy, apolitical nation. Just as before WWII, with Press and media oblivious to the danger, supposedly the 'Voice of the People', yet no criticism or revealment of the truth ever appears in Press or BBC (in debt heavily, to the European Bank). Why are they so guilty of hiding the truth about the takeover of Britain by GEU? Are they in cohesion with the Labour Government? There is an obvious plot to keep the people in ignorance of this shameful handover of Britain to an undemocratic German-controlled EU leading us into a communist–style dictatorship, with total loss of the freedom and sovereignty we have gained and held by patriotic vigilance.

In 1995 Mrs Thatcher said in Parliament: *"You have not anchored Germany to Europe; you have anchored Europe to a newly dominant, unified Germany"*, how far-seeing! Now in German control, as yet in shape unrealised by the victims, caught in a net of German deceit and empty promises, inexorably leading to complete mastery. As the USSR faded into history, overtaken by the new KGB dictatorship, Germany, under its EU cloak, was already on its planned path to overtake America, with the size and growth of its extended economic values.

In May 1997, Roman Herzog (former German President), receiving the International Charlemagne Prize for his efforts to unite Europe, admitted the truth:

"*Charlemagne, himself, sought the unification of Europe* – the truth must be told, *only by wading through a sea of blood, sweat and tears,* did he reach it. Germany has been Europe's greatest perpetrator, instigating that bloodshed." One wonders how Tony Blair came to be chosen for this prize? Joschka Fischer (ex Communist, now Leader of the Green Party) said:

"*Germany needs NOT democracy, but a system of Statecraft, similar to that of the Soviet dictatorship,* enabling the German political and military élite to organise Europe's industrial capacity, and the military qualities of German people or revival of the German race, *Europe is just an extension of Germany.*" That said it all, with Fischer in typical German self-worship.

Yugoslavia was deliberately undermined by BND (German Intelligence Service *[Bundesnachrichtendienst]*) under Klaus Kinkel, throughout 1980, using German agents working with former Croatian Fascists, close allies of Hitler (providing needed outlet to the Adriatic). *Germany finally destroyed the multi-ethnic state of Yugoslavia, arranging the breakaway of Catholic Croatia and Slovenia.* Marshal Tito established a new

Constitution for Yugoslavia, creating a new Federal Republic, which lasted over 30 years, until Germany broke it, and arranged a more compliant leader under her control. Once again Anglo-Americans have been fooled by German trickery.

German machinations in the Balkans in WWI were repeated in WWII. Yugoslavia, historical ally of Britain against German imperialism, has now been broken up into the same religious and racial statelets the Nazis established Croatia, Slovenia, Bosnia had their own Nazi Waffen SS divisions. In 1991 Germany, followed by the Vatican, recognised Croatia, which massacred one million Serbs, gypsies and Jews at Jasenovac concentration camp. The wartime Archbishop Stepinac, whose own priests helped run the extermination camp, was beatified by the previous Pope in 2002!

Albania was favoured by NATO as an ally of Germany, whilst operating the biggest drug and gun-running corridor through Kosovo and Tiranen. Germany gained control by outright purchase of their main asset, their chromite mines. *Albanians,* in the historical Serb province of *Kosovo,* who had conducted massive ethnic cleansing of Serbs over the previous 100 years, (with help of Nazis during the war and Tito thereafter), were now armed by Germany as *Freedom Fighters* (for whose Freedom?). Provoked by repeated terrorist attacks by Kosovo Freedom Fighters, the anticipated Serb response gave German-controlled Europe the excuse to lead NATO into an illegal war against a sovereign state – by cunning German contrivance. This served Germany's historical aim of destroying Serbia, gaining so-called German territory in the East, thus helping construction of German Europe, now EU. Similarly, with Macedonia the EU cleverly had NATO do all the donkey work, transforming it into a vassal state of EU. So, if things go wrong, NATO will be blamed: Thus another smart German manoeuvre.

In WWII one million Serbs were massacred by Croation fascists, with one million displaced because of Germany's aggressive interference and plotting. In 1991 Germany unilaterally recognised Croatia and Slovenia as separate sovereign states, completing her astutely conceived domination of the Baltic with 4,000 German troops in Croatia, the first deployment of German troops since WWII, to help enforce the so-called 'Peace Agreement'. All part of Germany's deep plan for overall control of all Europe, both West and East. At the same time, settling old scores of WWII.

The agricultural economy collapsed in the rest of Eastern Europe because the EU prevents their exports to the West. Their media, business and agricultural land are being acquired by Western European business, mainly German. Just as the Nazis planned in the 1930s, the national states of Europe, for whose freedom Britain and America fought two bloody wars, sacrificing their heroic young men, effectively, no longer exist as self-governing entities. The aftermath of WWII, with Germany now established as the strongest force in Europe. In fact, the German-led EU is becoming an exact reproduction of that obnoxious mixture of German aggressive imperialism and continental fascism, against which we were forced to fight. Thus the European Union, spells danger to World Peace, undermining Anglo-American costly post-war efforts, and contributions to true peace and harmony.

Germany, as Strongman of Europe, has again seen to the split-up of Czechoslovakia, annexed by Hitler, in Germany's War, establishing a 'Sudeten Fund' to allow Germans, dismissed post-war for collaboration with the Nazis in WWII, in their brutal oppression of the Czech people, now to return to the shamefully carved-up Czech Republic, although such action was forbidden by the Allies. Further proof that Germany refuses to accept the rules of War, even when totally defeated, under fully signed agreements, ever seeking her own cunning way round.

In other words, Germany is now intent on winning the Battle of the Peace, having failed to win by War, wholesale murder and brutal bloodshed, now by even more cunning, deceitful means. Instead of concentrating solely on rebuilding its empire by military strength, Germany has a new master plan, through economic means. First by buying an empire, using the strength of its business community. German major industry which remained basically strong post-war, by secret arrangements with Nazi leaders from 1943 (with defeat in sight), was now reinvigorated through American dollars, by Adenauer's deceit, followed by the American Banks' super-generosity of the Marshall plan; basically anti-Communist, (America's main fear in Europe). Thereby rebuilding German strength and aggression. At amazing speed, German industry gathered strength with the addition of the business framework of those Nazi leaders who fled through the Vatican 'rat-lines' and other means, with hoards of stolen wealth boasting the World's Third largest national economy, Germany now surpassed England in the economic area.

Thus the huge Deutsche Bank bought America's Bankers Trust, 1998, creating the world's largest financial services company. Germany's leading companies: Allianz, Daimler, Hoechst, Krupp, Thyssen, Siemens, I.G. Farben, all still there, where a large German contingent was ready to hand.

The Dresdner Bank bought U.S. Wasserstein Pirella & Co. for $1.6 billion dollars – gaining their extensive client lists, including Phillip Morris and Time Warner. Daimler Benz bought the Chrysler Corporation for over $37 billion dollars, becoming the biggest builder of truck engines, and the foremost manufacturer of commercial vehicles in the world – and the second largest exporter of military hardwear. In 1998 Thyssen Krupp merged as Europe's largest, and the world's third largest steel producer. German insurance giant Allianz paid $33 million dollars for Pimco Advisors Holdings, Europe's second largest insurer. BMW and Daimler-Benz have a major plant in Tuscalooza, Alabama. In September 2000 RWE bought British major Thames Water for $4.3 billion dollars. RWE bought British American Waterworks, and other power companies.

At long last in 2001 there arose loud objections on the basis of national security, at giving away America's telecommunications to German foreigners. Somebody, finally, must have smelled danger. Where does Germany obtain all these extensive, huge piles of money, for such massive purchases, especially of key American and British Banks and power units? Germany keeps raising her sights and bidding for major strategic Banks, power plants, water, electricity, railway controls in America especially, and also Britain, costing huge billions of dollars. The Blair Government seriously considered an offer from Germany's State-owned Bank, West L.B., for Railtrack's 2,300 miles of track and 2,500 stations, including the Channel Tunnel Rail link. Railtrack owns Britain's railway infrastructure, including stations, tracks, signals, tunnels, bridges, viaducts etc. What a dangerous weapon to put into the hands of our everlasting enemy Germany! As an ex WWII warrior and Intelligence officer, it makes my hackles rise. As Churchill said: "Nothing but a change of the German heart can avert another catastrophe, unlikely to come from within, for the true German nature has never changed". "The Germans, after all, had been belligerent for 2000 years." (Willliam Manchester biography).

Yet the West is so trusting, and easily fooled by the arch liars and deceivers and tricksters – from Lenin to Gobachëv and the KGB, from the earliest Germani to Goebbels, who carried on the Leninist policy that lies, lies, lies, if often enough repeated, will be believed. Unlike us, Germany protects herself, first and foremost, holding firmly to her sovereignty and ever-growing possessions. The difference lies in her cunning new approach, in that insatiable quest for power. Buying a well planned Empire from trusting enemies, whilst protecting her own. When they have completed the circle, consolidating their global economic power and building total encirclement of Europe and the East, with the fast-enclosing EU Superstate, economic and military power, we may expect their threatened *Blitzkrieg,* To assume full command and control in the carefully prepared, domineering dictatorship – unless chaos intervenes again.

German powerful RWE busily buying British and American waterworks, major-size Thames Water and New Jersey base of Water Works Co. Inc. and now penetrating other overseas markets including Australia and Chile, in their attack on strategic utility companies. The American Water Works is the largest and most diversified, publicly traded water services company in the U.S. This acquisition will give RWE presence in 44 countries on 6 continents, serving a population of 56 million. Strategic implications warrant a command position to Germany for any nation in dispute with them. A highly dangerous position! America take heed!

Why no protecting screen, to prevent industry yielding control of the basic resources upon which our nations depend for daily operations and survival? Quick profits may put nations in danger, with the people paying the penalty, as always, for their appointed leaders' lack of security. RWE is expanding its uncontrolled efforts, to embrace gas and electricity and power generation and distribution facilities – even including waste management. Water is not only the world's greatest and most necessary commodity, but is also steadily declining in availability. Just consider the terrible threat to our nation's safety and security, now delivered into the unfriendly hands of ill-wishers. The London *Times* on 2nd July 2001 wrote on the EU power of Brussels stating: "Washington is aware that the European Union has a hidden anti-U.S. agenda".

German EU now interferes with internal U.S. company sales and purchases. GEU seeks to protect European businesses from foreign competition – by well-trained EU officials. *Germany has passed a law refusing such transactions within Germany.* What may this mean for the future, with Germany controlling EU and a major part of the world? World history proves that Germany may never be trusted, even with agreed, signed and sealed contracts or treaties, from the Assyrians to Hitler. Will our Statesmen ever learn their most important duties and responsibility for the safety and security of their people, who put them into office to provide such protection? The Nazi bombs of WWII raining down on helpless, innocent people and the Muslim fanatics' evil treachery of 11th September 2001, still continuing relentlessly in Britain, surely should suffice to make them scent danger? England is now under constant threat, even from Muslims born in this country, but under continuous fanatical influence.

German Acquisitions: (General List)

Table A - US Businesses

Name	Type of Business	Acquired by
Airborne Express	Air courier/airport	Deutsche Bank
American Water Works	Water utility supplier	RWE
Arista	Record company	BMG Entertainment
Bankers Trust	Bank	Deutsche Bank
Chrysler	Automotive	Daimler-Benz
DHL	WorldwideAir courier	Deutsche Bank
Doubleday	Publisher	Bertelsmann
Farrar, Straus & Giroux	Publisher	Holtzbrinck
Fireman's Fund	Insurance	Allianz
Henry Holt	Publisher	Holtzbrinck
Marion Merril Dow Chem	Pharmaceutical	Aventis
MEMC Electronic Mtls	Silicon wafers	E.ON AG
PIMCO Advisors Holdings	Investment advisory	Allianz
Random House	Publisher	Bertelsmann
RCA	Record company	BMG Entertainment
Shared Medical Systems	Medical	Siemens
St. Martin's Press	Publisher	Holtzbrinck
TopTier Software Inc.	Portal software developer	SAP AG
VoiceStream	WirelessCommunication	Deutsche Telekom
Westinghouse Electric Co	Power supplier	Siemens
Windham Hill	Record company	BMG Entertainment
Zurich Scudder	Investment Manager	Deutsche Bank

Table B - UK Businesses

Name	Type of Business	Acquired by
Boots Pharmaceuticals	Pharmaceuticals	BASF
Cornhill Insurance	Insurance	Allianz
Grattan Mail Order	Mail order	Otto Versand
Kleinwort Benson	Global investment banking	Dresdner Bank
Lansing	Forklift Manufacturing	Linde
Lloyds Chemist	Pharmacy chain	Gehe
Morgan Grenfell	Bank	Deutsche Bank
One2One Mobiles	Communication	Deutsche Telecom
Plessey	Digital communication	Siemens
Powergen	Electricity & gas provider	(pending) E.ON AG
Midland Electricity	Electricity & gas provider	(pending) E.ON

Rolls-Royce	Automotive & aviation	Volkswagen
Highland Energy	Electricity	RWE
Innogy	Electricity	EON
Thames Water	Water utility supplier	RWE
Thomas Cook	Travel	WestLB

Table C - Others

Name	Type of Business	Acquired by
Czech Gas monopoly	Gas	RWE
Hungary Gas	Gas	50% RWE
Polish Energy	Electricity and Gas	85% RWE

Germany is now Buying and Building her Fourth Empire, using EU as cloak – with acquisitions in every conceivable industry. Making enormous growth in global power for the Reich! America's great industrial and military power, allied to Britain's fighting strength and military ability next-to-none, have twice denied Germany's dictatorial global conquest and power. Now America and Britain are Germany's prime target – for, as history proves, they never forget and never forgive each defeat – working tenaciously towards the next attempt, convinced that they are destined to control and command Europe and the world, as dictators unopposed. Churchill said "The Germans, after all, had been belligerent for 2000 years". "They never change." How soon his words of wisdom and warning are forgotten. Europe's leaders may not even fully understand what the German EU (GEU) is about. From 1999 to 2001 German companies took over 2,779 U.S. companies (worth $766 billion dollars) in an economic *Blitzkrieg:* How were such sales and so much money contrived? With American Banks and Industrialists' support, led, admittedly, by Rockefeller.

When John Major was signing the Maastricht Treaty, he needed an opt-out from acceptance of the Euro. He weakly bargained diplomatic recognition of the seceding Yugoslav states, as Germany's price. The German Foreign Minister remarked: "By this, Germany has regained diplomatically everything lost in Eastern Europe as the result of two world wars". Such was the atrocious weakness of Major's leadership of Britain. Thank God we had not to suffer his 'leadership' in war! Margaret Thatcher would have rejected the connived Maastricht Treaty and all the German wiles. He sold Devonport Dockyard, our main military and nuclear port to

Dick Cheney's Haliburton Corporation for peanuts, gaining as reward MD Europe of the Bush family's Carlyle Weapons, receiving $1 million per annum for lifetime.

Clearly, Germany's policy is simply Domination, as always, reproducing her old concentric circles model for global domination, with Germany as world-centre, controlling every radius. And yet our own leaders still seem unaware, despite all the facts, clearly revealed, of each move made by Germany, with Nazi leaders going 'Underground' before War-end to plan recovery, and prepare for the next war. Only this time, having learnt from all those repeated defeats, they are now operating, not only successfully, but even with our befooled help, as "useful idiots", in Lenin's telling mockery, to win decisively the Battle of the Peace by strategic economic means, while at the same time, secretly rebuilding her military strength. And our befooled Leaders successively and continuously support GEU. We lack our Churchill to rescue us from encirclement! Our MPs fail to scent their personal danger as well as the fate of Parliament when Brussels becomes Superstate centre. Their numbers will diminish rapidly, so they are, in fact, voting themselves out of job and future!

On the 1994 anniversary of the Nazi brutally devastating attack on Poland, a German Minister said: "If integration (=expansion) in Eastern Europe were not to proceed, a future German government might be called upon, or compelled by its own security considerations, to solve the problems of the area on its own and in traditional manner".

Germany's powers of deceit and corruption even outdo the classic Lenin model. In WWII, The Union Bank of Switzerland and Credit Suisse, regarded by the world as impermeable, totally neutral and trustworthy to all-comers, actually collaborated in depth with the Axis Powers – a world betrayal! Hitler's personal wealth and looted Jewish treasures, gold and diamonds and cash, kept in UBS, with Mussolini's stolen loot in Credit Suisse. Swiss banks funded the Nazi war machine. Switzerland acted as spy centre and channel for secret negotiations. Instead of welcoming refugees, as they pretended, they actually turned back thousands to worse fate. Post-war Swiss banks for years refused to hand over money entrusted to their safe-keeping by Jewish clients from Germany. Switzerland has now brought its economic practices into conformity with EU, to enhance their international competitiveness, signing agreements in 1991 in Bern and Brussels, further to liberalise trade ties. Almost 80% of Swiss imports come from EU with 31% from Germany. They may no longer be regarded as neutral, but now decidedly pro-Germany, pro-EU.

Now joined by France's giant Aerospatiale-Matra, Germany's Daimler Chrysler Aerospace (DASA) and Spain's CASA, in Europe's Aeronautic Defence and Space Company (EADC) in a group of some 96 million employees and annual turnover of $1 billion dollars. One wonders what and where is Britain, still busily disarming and even now drastically reducing her Forces. Jane's *Defence Weekly* of 15/12/1999 wrote: "EADC is undoubtedly the driving force in Europe – and has the inner strength to become Global leaders". Rolls Royce, once proudly British, now belongs to German Volkswagen. Rudolph Scharping, Germany's Defence Minister, re common defence capability, has called for Europe to set up a joint airtransport command – to ensure Europe's ability to undertake military action round the WORLD – thus reducing reliance on the U.S.A. In fact the EU has assembled a massive conglomerate, which will put it to the fore in military strategy, leaving America and Britain far behind in world leadership.

In 1995 Bernard Connolly (*"Rotten Heart of Europe"*) outlined the EU system as a "Trojan horse", used as a dangerous cloak for German ambitions. It was the German decision to create RRF (Rapid Retaliation Force), independent of NATO. Unfortunately the Americans could not see the danger signals, indicated from Germany, with her permanent over-arching aggression plan (cleverly cloaked under EU), for total mastery of greater Europe from the Atlantic to the Urals. Churchill said: *"All will seek is the illusion of peace"*. So we did, and America certainly suffered the illusion of a cured Germany (as certainly with Japan), become more ally than enemy. When, in fact Germany was seeking a long-range policy of close co-operation with the East. Thus, by following the factual fulfilment of Lenin's scheme, to destroy the nation state by collectivist merging of nations, Germany would realise her own full nationalistic and racial potential – always leaning towards Russia.

Key Features of German Deceit

In 1992, France became bound to Russia, as her agreed agent, to bring Russia into an extended European Federation – to promote collective security. In 1990 Professor Herzog denigrated the nation state, publicly identifying with Lenin's objective. The *Maastricht Treaty* then deprived

EU nation states of key elements of their sovereignty; their currency, internal and external security, transferred, for the first time, to a European institution. Signed for Britain by a disloyal Prime Minister John Major (against strong advice and warning), saying we are all European citizens now, including our Queen, as Mrs Windsor, just another European citizen. The people's permission was not sought and there was no discussion. No wonder millions left his Party in disgust, followed by a complete collapse of Government at the following General Election, in disgrace for over a decade, he was followed by Blair who surrendered completely to GEU.

Yet America's materialistic world still seemed oblivious of the frightening reality, of the concealed intentions of this menacing, reborn German fast-growing giant, with huge secret resources immediately available. Though the German Mark became worthless post-war, and the Black Market ruled a bargaining scene, until we created their new currency Mark in 1997/8, as I witnessed. So, whence came this sudden huge wealth? Where was it all stored in the Nazi era? Who financed Germany's fantastic buying power, unmatched by all other states together? I presume American/German Banks and Rockefeller organisation et al. just as they helped to finance Adolf Hitler. We shall examine their peculiar world organisation activities later.

Meanwhile, German military is rebuilding fast and secretly as in 1920s/30s, using pseudo peace-keeping roles, as excuse. Playing a devious role in Kosovo, Croatia, being helpful in supplying peace-keeping troops, all undergoing strict home training. The old German trickery is still there, as deceitful and two-forked as ever. Adept at convincing lies, matching those of its Leninist/KGB trained ally, at the devil's trade of deceit, into which the West easily falls, trusting victim, always with America, especially, in their sights (as also Britain), whilst proffering friendship. Now both the KGB-led Russian dictatorship and the GEU Superstate, are seeking global power and world-domination by pseudo-peaceful means, using every trick in their training. These are aimed specifically at America and Britain, both economically and militarily.

Britain's so called "New Labour" Government has recklessly thrown in its lot with German-led Europe. America has fallen prey to every conceivable form of espionage in the 20/21st century from Russia, China, the East, Asia and the Arab world. Finally it is learning fast not to put its trust in erstwhile 'Friends' in Europe, from France to Arabia, and to trade for its own well-protected and insured benefit, with trustworthy, proven allies, balancing gains and losses. Thus America is now considering closure of well-established military bases in Germany, so useful and profitable to the Germans.

Germany has been allowed, by its so readily trusting American friends, to establish a permanent military facility at Alamagordo, New Mexico, with (scarcely credible), an open-skies treaty for German planes flying over and surveying (and mapping) in totem. Something which needs 100% secrecy for complete safety. Even sharing training and joint military exercises – for German identification records. Like Samson giving away the secret of his great strength – with resultant downfall, to his undoing. America should now look closely to her security. The Chinese were able to obtain all U.S. classified, most sensitive military, technical and nuclear information (painstakenly developed and built up over many years of highest quality operations, by most qualified American and British staff of highly trained experts – at tremendous cost and outstanding success) – simply by tapping into unguarded U.S. computer, technical system, without restriction and with minimum effort. Thus China, in quick time, learnt all U.S. secrets and was able to construct her own copies of U.S. nuclear warheads, with all technical know-how, and sell them on! Enough to make strong men weep! But America has the resilience to ride its body-blows and restore terms with China, now building her own industrial and military strength as a world power.

American nuclear bombs are in new WMD storage vaults in EU states, with many in Germany. The EU possesses hundreds of nuclear bombs. Germany has an advanced science and technology base, capable of supporting a nuclear programme. This needs careful assessment for future consideration. Our British/American defence organisations seem to have no conception of this ongoing, tremendous build-up of power – with the sole aim of the creation of a *Superstate Dictatorship* with total world control. Whilst we continue to reduce our Armed Forces and equipment, Germany is quickly building hers (see later Bundeswehr totality), with Europe providing the rest. Their intention is clearly to *reduce NATO* and then do away with it, leaving GEU in full power and able to argue with, if not threaten, America, with once 'Great' Britain now reduced to Third World status.

KGB trained Putin does not favour NATO expansion in the East under German EU pressure: *"Our relations with the West have moved backwards since the events in the Balkans"*. Russia is now seeking to establish a quasi-Soviet bloc, by promoting racial and religious statelets within their former satellites, Chechnya and Georgia, and suppressing sovereignty in an economic supernational bloc. Lenin said: "Federation is a transitional form towards complete union of all nations". He was cleverer and even nastier than the Germans, who learnt much of their trickery from him. Gobachëv and Yeltsin followed Lenin very comprehensively by devising persuasive bilateral agreements with EU countries, using spies and agents to winkle out detailed information. Stephen Koch speaking in 1994 said: "A Communist must be prepared to resort to all sorts of schemes as stratagems, employ illegitimate methods, conceal truth and lie for the revolution!" Lies convince and open doors. It is a special art.

The Soviet saw anti-fascism as "strategic eyewash for fools." Golitzyn: "Leninist strategic deception determines Soviet behaviour at all times". Victor Savorov (a defector): "Stalin's real aim = facilitate such a conflagration in Europe, involving Germany, France and Britain, that not only would European empires be decapitated, but the Soviet Revolution would be free to seize total hegemony throughout Europe by filling the resultant power vacuum". Adenauer and Stresemann were both past masters of dialectical diplomatic double-talk. In 1946 Adenauer was in America preaching the need for a *United Europe*, with Press support. The U.S. Pentagon, totally convinced by Adenauer, suggested 50 divisions for a new German Army to combat the Soviet growing menace. The Plan for a United Europe, cleverly fed to America, was just a re-hash of the old Pan-German aspiration for a German-dominated Europe – gaining Germany full power. The returned Nazis *Hochschule für Politik* in Berlin, Munich, Dusseldorf, were modelled on Leninist lines. Also 'Research Institutes' spawned by the Soviet Academy of Sciences, were progressing Lenin's doctrine of dialectic deceit.

The German General Staff were reformed, aiming to conquer Europe, by *first isolating and neutralising and reducing the British. "Only then may we expand to the East."* Germany's clandestine, devious two-sided plans depended essentially upon American support and their inability to see through German cunning proposals: "Rebuild Germany as bulwark against the East" – exactly as post-war Nazis envisaged with Germany's great capacity for intrigue and duplicity. American policy makers were quickly persuaded by German pan-Europeanism, convinced by Germany's calculated lies, turning truth on its head. Nazi policymakers' objective was to establish a new European Union on Federalist basis – following Lenin's thesis: *"Federation is a traditional form towards complete union of all nations"* – under their domination.

Objective: turn EU into a community of related peoples, with the *final aim of creating a new German Reich. Then abandon the euro for Deutschmark for ALL EU.* With EU thus dependent on Germany, economically and politically, with the European Central Bank in Frankfurt gaining financial control. Thus Third Reich's ambition of imposing a Single Currency on the whole of Europe now realised and in complete German command: Fourth Reich; Planned for the future total mastery.

The pre-agreed German/Soviet Partition of Central Europe includes a Commonwealth between Germany, Bohemia and Moravia, agreed by the Soviets in September 1990 at Geneva – through break-up of the Czech Republic, to be incorporated into Germany. The Soviets also agreed to the division of Yugoslavia, with Croatia and Slovenia under German economic influence. Germany agreed full Russian control of: Ukraine, Latvia and Estonia. Both agreed to the restoration of Hungary within the previous borders of 1920. Thus carving up Europe between them to joint satisfaction. But the Soviets were not prepared to accept Germany's planned model of European hegemony, centred on Berlin, with Russia banished to an Asian no-man's land beyond the Urals. *The Soviets had their own future plans, westward to the Atlantic, well concealed from everybody especially the Germans.* (cf. Christopher Story: *The European Union Collective*).

The ECJ (European Court of Justice) major plan of EU, successfully destabilised the British legal system by developing the EU concept of *corpus juris*, completely foreign to English Common Law – Britain's greatest gift to the world – now totally undermined by GEU intent. Thus destroying the basic foundation of Britain's self-contained independence and freedom under its own laws. *The European Legal Area Project, managed by the European Commission, is the most lethal of all threats to Britain's most ancient and hallowed liberties,* fought by the British to maintain over many generations, and respected throughout the world, whose main legal systems are based on the British. ECJ is Europe's High Court, ensuring that, on signing a Treaty, the State implements all facets. *Laws created by Brussels and administered by ECJ will supersede the sovereign laws of member nations.* The ECJ is the undisputed final judge of EC law. Member states, on signing, have ceded the power of their national courts to the Luxembourg based ECJ. While British law relies on precedent (judges rulings), establishing consistency in the application of law over the years. EU, by contrast, is immediate, bound by no custom or practice.

There is a threat to British national sovereignty, forced by EU changes in beliefs, standards and judicial institutions. The dangerous reality is that all powers turned over to EU institutions are permanently subject to European Community law, and therefore removed from the ambit of national legislation. The German-led EU policy of transforming power through treaties (as a change from war), over the past 50 years, has been more effective in damaging Britain than Hitler's all-out attack in WWII. The UK now faces the ultimate danger of the loss of our national identity we have defended through bitter wars, principally of German aggression. Our politicians lack the courage of conviction of the warriors who fought against well-nigh impossible odds for liberty and freedom of our Country under our own sovereignty and British laws.

The original drive for European integration split into two broad camps, the 'federalists' (called intergovernmentalists), and the functionalists (for supranation states), including two ideologically competitive elements: the Council and the Commission, each vying for power and control, making tension between them. The Council of Ministers is but an interim measure to become swallowed up in the functionalist Commission. Thus integration, step by step, by means of added treaties provided inconsistencies and anomalies, called *engreinage* or 'beneficial crisis', copying the Leninist method. Although apparently a new form of integration of these two forms, it is basically neo-functionalist, and thus antidemocratic. In fact Spinelli foretold its future clearly as *dictatorship* – a clear vision of the final development to come – denying people the right to determine their own destinies. Interposing the dictatorship of the technocrats, who alone are capable of deciding what is good for the "People." Thus, rule by Technocrats (once called civil servants) now become the masters, in this dictatorship.

The role of elected officials and representatives, is solely to act as spokesmen for their masters, to help them gain added power in a thinly covered veneer of 'democracy', disguising the truth from the people, that they are now subject to a fundamentally anti-democratic process. As for law, the true role of the ECJ is not to dispense justice but, in a parody of the rule of law, to cement the dominance of the technocrats overall.

Many MEPs actually believe, once elected, that they are truly democratic, highly paid, representatives of the people. Form is confused with substance, for they are to be seen, overpaid and over indulged – but not heard. Any speech permitted cannot exceed 90 seconds. They are, in fact, used as hugely overpaid ghosts, to play a minor role, lacking substance – a deceit. The real power lies with the supranational authority, in the form of the unelected Commission, whose power, jealously guarded, is exercised through its exclusive right to propose new legislation. Called "conditional agenda setting", this monopoly enables it to set the agenda, keeping up the speed of integration. Continuous proposals must be created by the Council (and the European Parliament for co-decisions) to maintain bewildered conformity, allowing no time to debate or consider, just obey without question.

Legislation is a one-way ratchet. All powers surrendered by member states pass into the *acquis communautaire*, never to be returned. The *acquis* is the inviolable, unarguable, criminal concept of EU "law," the foundation of the integration process, the irrefutable weapon of the Commission until the process is finalised – giving the Commission total control. What enters the *acquis* can never be returned. Thus the power of debate of formerly independent sovereign states is finally removed. Politicians become the servants of the Commission, not of the people and must do their bidding, acting as agents, without argument, or attempt to negotiate. Many member states have voluntarily, or by political force, fallen into the dragnet of the EU. Succumbing to the Leninist doctrine of persuade and rule by a pyramid of lies and deception.

In the "The Breakdown of Europe", Sir Richard Body said: "Before we allow ourselves to be dragged any further down a European road, whose direction was set by the idealists of the `1950s, we should rub our eyes, wake up and recognise what kind of a world we are really going to be living in a few years from now". A sentiment I heartily endorse.

Corpus Juris is defined by Michael Shrimpton as "the embryo of a future European Criminal Code, a blue print for rationalising Europe's criminal laws and forming a single European Legal Area". This would involve sweeping away the existing criminal justice systems of the member states. Trial by Jury and *habeas corpus* would be abolished, with *our ancient freedoms, to be replaced by an inquisitorial system based on the tyrannical Napoleonic Code*. The presumption of innocence would become worthless, and every man, woman and child liable to arrest at the whim of the European Public Prosecutor. The heart of *Corpus Juris* is the provision for detention without trial, initially up to six months, renewable without limit of time. Suspects could remain locked up for years without evidence being shown, or without a public hearing-held incommunicado.

Our Common Law applies as much to the state and its officials as it does to the individuals. Corpus Juris is about the destruction of our legal system, our national sovereignty, and the abolition forever of Habeas Corpus and Trial by Jury. It would end our Magna Carta and Rule of Law and, above all, our independence. The best way of staying out of this grimly threatening European Legal Area, is by leaving the EU.

Neither Nazism nor the EU is any way democratic! Yet the EU's deviously conceived agenda is supported by well-intentioned people believing they are acting in the best interests of Britain, and the citizens of Europe in general. They assume that they have the right to tell us what is best for us – thus posing as great a danger to our liberty, as formerly convinced supporters of the Nazis. They possess all the resources, at their disposal, of their member states, including their police and prisons and state-sanctioned violence to enforce their' good intentions': Shades of the prophesying "*1984*".

"Citizens" of Europe will eventually wake up to the hard truth, that they are no longer in control of their own destinies. As history shows, it will all end in violent rebellion and bloodshed – where it all began. To quote Nietzsche again: "The German is an expert on secret paths to chaos". Using those same skills of dexterous deceit and cunning, refined by their new secret collaboration with the USSR, especially the accepted master of deceit, Lenin, they have used new tactics. After the failure of direct war and military might in successive wars, they have discovered the new tool, ready to hand, of the European Union. Behind this comfortable cloak, they have developed their cunning new plans of conquest. First by building an Empire by purchase of major units of power in America and Britain primarily, but also elsewhere, expanding both West and East. As the overall strength of EU and under its useful guise, they have now reached the *power-control point of Greater Europe, with the production of the EU Con/Treaty, on the verge of acceptance not only in Europe generally, but especially in Britain, their prime target.* The present Labour Government, is seeking to slide it through almost in entirety, without allowing the British people the right of vote, for or against, in a Referendum.

They rely upon the general state of apathy towards politics in modern

Britain, with the connivance of the main body of the Press and media (including the BBC and ITV and major political parties), In fact, cunningly, the people have been kept unaware of all that has been done, "in their name", against Britain and the British people until that same, stubborn, freedom-loving people discover how they have been betrayed – and rise up, as they have done in past history, to overthrow these tyrants, who seek to rob Britain of her sovereignty and turn her into a vassal state, powerless under the European Superstate, before final total domination by Germany in their planned dictatorship. In fact the GEU is a reproduction of that obnoxious mixture of German imperialism and continental fascism which Britain and America defeated in two World Wars, at great sacrifice of our brave young men and women, plunging our Western world into costly chaos.

Now, 60 years later, in 2008, that heroic United Kingdom effectively no longer exists. *Westminster Parliament is subordinate to the European Commission in Brussels,* whose ever-growing purposeful confusion of the outpouring of over 111,000 often stupid, regulations (each with the strength of law, undeniable and unalterable under this unchangeable *acquis communautaire)* now not only bypass our Parliament, but also force our Parliament to carry out their orders at our expense. So we are directed in absolute detail, by unelected bureaucrats, to absurdity and stunned disbelief. But this continuous flow of regulations, orders and direction is of a purpose, to keep us all fully occupied in minutiae, without time to pause and reflect on the hidden, evil corruption of our ancient freedom and sovereignty.

The British Law Courts must obey the "Superior" European Court of Justice in Strasbourg, whose declared political task: is to further the "integration" (i.e. abolition) of the once-free nation states of Europe – i.e. it is not a Court in the English sense, but every day it makes unrevocable law for the present EU "nations". British people may now be extradited to any European country, without our natural protection under English common law of *"habeas corpus"* or trial by jury. However, German citizens, by contrast, cannot be extradited anywhere. In other words, they are making European laws but do not have to abide by them! The German hand is on the tiller, under the guise of the European Union, but as ever, follows only its own desired direction.

The *Nice Treaty* made it possible, dictator fashion, to ban any political parties in any European country not approved by the shadowy leaders of EU. In Eastern Europe the erstwhile Czechoslovakia, annexed by Hitler, has now been broken up again in Germany's favour – now the Strongman of Europe. Germany has established a "Sudeten Fund" to allow Germans, expelled post-war for collaboration with the Nazis in their brutal oppression of the Czechs, now to return to the mangled Czech Republic – although expressly forbidden by the Allies. Thus the regulations laid down by the Allies, and accepted by Germany are now being turned on their heads and ignored by present Germany, carrying on their reputation of breaking agreements and contracts to suit themselves.

Britain is staring into the abyss. Unless we take the necessary, deliberate action to stop this evil plan, now nearing the point of no return, we stand to lose all we have fought for and tenaciously held-our sovereignty and our freedom under British law and rule, to pursue our lives with full liberty. The lives and liberty of our children and future generations are now at stake, depending on our determined action to stop this invasion before it is too late. We must now move on to examine our present situation in 2008, on the brink of finalisation of this rehashed Constitution— resoundingly refused in a Referendum in 2005 by French and Dutch people, now cunningly retitled as Treaty, but actually that identical Constitution, with one or two slight changes to convince (or confuse) us. I name it the Con/Treaty, German inspired.

Pretending to act for the general good in a community of 'equals', their target is eventually revealed: first an EU Superstate, en route deviously to become a German dominated Dictatorship. We are coerced and invited to yield our sovereignty, ancient rights and hard-won Freedom to become, for the first time in our long history, a vassal state under the German jack - boot. WWI and WWII should have taught us the brutal German reality. Their success has been financed and promoted from outside plutocratic secret sources (as was Hitler's), with hidden aims, with their own secret plans of world control and World Government — from the illuminati to the Fabians and other concealed organisations in Britain, Europe and America of the supremely wealthy and dangerous. Hence Germany's acquired financial power, enabling her to expand by economic acquisi- tions beyond the scope of other states, in many directions including her greatest ever military development. Germany has now achieved her long- sought dominance of Europe, West and East, and is steadily advancing further, with her old aggressive tactics showing clearly.

Bundeswehr (German Armed Forces)

In November 1955, the Bundeswehr (German Armed Forces), became 'officially established', with USA approval, for the defence of Germany's borders. Only 10 years after War end, despite the conditions laid down by Churchill and Roosevelt. In fact, professional troops were already secretly in training, lacking only full armaments. Soon Germany 'obligingly' offered help to overstretched NATO forces, with German unarmed soldiers for peace-keeping purposes. Acceptance set the quick expansion of her Armed Forces, with arms training and secret re-armament.

Conscription of 17 to 45 year olds began in 1956 and has continued ever since, supplying over 50,000 annually, trained conscripts and thousands of active reservists, thus building a massive reserve force ready to fill all requirements. As the only country maintaining conscription, with the biggest Armed Forces, next to America, what is the need for such continuous build-up, with NATO so well established, and EU demanding its own Standing Army?

During the Cold War, the Bundeswehr supplied NATO's needs, gradually working their build-up to becoming the major defence force in Central and Eastern Europe, with 495,000 military and 20,000 civilian personnel. With Tanks and APCs, trucks, combat aircraft, air defence and Navy in the Baltic Approaches, gradually building bigger, stronger forces, well equipped

In 1990, after Germany's reunification, the Bundeswehr was reduced to 375,000, with the disbanded Volksarmee of East Germany (Russian Zone) joining the Bundeswehr in October as the "Armee der Einheit" (unity). The reshaped Bundeswehr now had some 350,000, trained, professional servicemen with full equipment. Plus 55,000 trained conscripts and thousands of active reservists, with over 75,000 civilian employees. 300,000 trained reservists are now available to their Armed Forces for service home and abroad. Some 15,000 women are also on active service, plus reservists.

In 1994 the defensive role of the Bundeswehr was redefined, now not only to protect Germany's borders, but also for 'crisis reaction and conflict prevention', now guarding Germany's security anywhere in the world, outside the borders of Germany, as part of NATO or EU, mandated by UN. The Joint Service Support Command was established in October 2000, including logistics and supporting function e.g military police and communications. Chief of Defence (CHOD) and Service Chiefs from Military Command: like Joint Chiefs of Staff USA.

Bundeswehr now among the world's most technologically advanced and equipped forces; engaged in international operations around the former Yugoslavia and Cambodia, Somalia, now serving in Afghanistan, Kosovo,, KFOR, Horn of Africa, Indian Ocean, Mediterranean, Sudan, Congo. They are also training Iraqi forces and others. Once again re-organising with their much extended strength as the greatest Armed Force in all Europe, second now only to America. They are buying 60 A400M transporters, plus 180 EF200 Fighter planes, tanks, corvettes, F125 class Frigates and 212 submarines. Ever expanding, whilst supporting the growth of EU Armed Forces. There is no explanation offered for this ever increasing Bundeswehr, at huge costs, impossible for other countries even to consider. Whence come the enormous funds needed to underwrite the vast costs continuously mounting? The Rockefeller Group seeking World Government.

Further German Military Initiatives: European Aeronautics Defence and Space Company: $25 million dollar contract for radar systems for global surveillance. Helicopters, transport aircraft and 4,000 command and special purpose vehicles. 180 Eurofighter jets (at $22 Billion dollars the costliest arms deal in history.) Next, operational equipment for the infantryman. The Frigate Sachsen, fitted with the most advanced armaments in German history (3 were ordered for delivery in 2005), with new air defence; 4 type 212A submarines-the most advanced ever built, a new Complex to be constructed outside Potsdam as HQ for EU-led operations. ThyssenKrupps bought Howaldwerke, the world's largest submarine builder. Also Deutsche-Werft, core of the European warship heavyweights (Frankfurter Allgcmein FAZ). KSK Germany's elite force (special forces command) now increased and integrated with NATOs Rapid Reaction Force.

Germany is now seeking a seat on the UN Security Council, which grants the power of veto. This high-speed aggressive Blitzkrieg rearming is manoeuvring Germany to the top position in Europe, making all others appear midgets in comparison. Done with a purpose to humiliate, bully, if not terrify other nations by her enormous strength and superiority. Thus able to dictate terms when desired. Sea Warriors: German Navy manoeuvres in the Baltic, trying out new combat techniques with units from 8 EU member states under German command. With Germany's Special Forces Commando (KSK) and Air Force participating. Meantime, the GEU is reducing British defence capability by expanding the service of British fighting forces in many combat zones stretched to capacity, with insufficient arms and protection gear, like the Land Rovers which are too vulnerable to bombs. Germany is now in the top position in Europe, dominating NATO and UN. So the trail is being carefully laid to German dictatorship or possibly a Third devastating War, with Britain fully stretched abroad, and undermanned at home.

The Bertlesmann Group

Germany's think tank and ex-officio voice, presaging and expounding German policy or embryo plans, with the necessary publicity. The World's second largest global media conglomerate, it owns Greenwood Press, Bantam, Random House Publishers and has merged with Pearson TV. This media giant has admitted it lied about its Nazi past, supporting Hitler and making huge profits from his regime, using Jewish slave labour in Germany, Latvia and Lithuania. Bertelsmann worked with the Nazi Propaganda Ministry, and printed 19 million books during WWII. Largest publisher for the Wehrmacht (Hitler's Armed Forces), in 1945 they lied to the Occupation Authorities, claiming they were closed down because of their resistance to the Nazis, but now admit it was solely due to shortage of paper. Their lies gained them their licence on which they have thrived ever since.

By 2006 Bertelsmann had 76,000 employees in books and magazines, publishing, film and music recording, on line services etc. With sales of 20 billion euros, they operate in USA, Europe, Germany, Australia etc. with a controlling stake in broadcasting across Europe. They even have a subsidiary company already administering some local authorities in England.

Venus Group was a high level network of security and defence experts across Europe, brought together (at Venusberg near Bonn) with the Bertelsmann Group for Policy Research in 2004, demanding a European Strategic Concept to meld into a single conceptual framework, national, civil and military, as well as offensive and defensive security and defence efforts ie promoting radical militarising of EU. They recommended substantial additions of military personnel and armaments' spending by ALL EU members, as necessary for world-wide military operations. A Supranational EU Defence Council, evading controls by all parliaments, would preside over planned wars, and direct military and civilian measures in all EU member states. A highly geared preparation for war at any time, anywhere.

EU Permanent Combined and Joint HQ to be established as responsibility of Trirectoire of Germany, France and Britain (overlooking Britain's alliance with America). An EU Counter-Terrorism Coordinator and EU Homeland Security Agency, with its own Minister to protect European security space.

What Europe Can and Cannot Do Now

1 – 1.75 million Europeans are now in uniform but only 170,000 are combat soldiers. Of these only 50,000, at the most, can be used for robust combat at any one time. European Security Strategy (ESS) policy: 1/. Increase trained and supported troops beyond 170,000.

2. Train other forces for follow-on missions e.g peace-keeping. EU to assume the responsibilities of a coalition leader: Strategic Intelligence essential, with advance communications and ground surveillance.

Gendarmerie, Guardia Civil and Carabinieri-type forces needed to bridge the gap between combat soldiering and the police, to establish civil society. French proposed 10,000. Specialists required for construction of infrastructure: sewage, water and electricity, to rebuild the Peace Eurogendfor established 18th October 2007 by Treaty governing the European Gendarmerie Force, starting in Bosnia-Herzegovina. Portugal, Turkey, Romania, Poland, Lithuania joined.

There is future danger for us, of being policed by a centrally commanded, unaccountable, heavily armed and militarised police force-the Eurogendarmerie and Europol, made up of foreigners (even Turks are to be recruited, as per the Treaty of Velsen), immune from prosecution whatever they do, subject to orders from Brussels only, so completely out of control of our Queen in Parliament. They will look like, feel like, act like, and actually be, a FORCE OF MILITARY OCCUPATION, tasked with subjugating the natives(us). It will be as if the Wehrmacht had successfully invaded and occupied us in 1940. Something our country has never seen since 1066. That is the German plan.

Increase of the hyper-regulation, strangling all private economic activity to the point where all business people, from the humblest shop keeper on the corner, right up to the Chairman of the biggest corporation in the city, has to go on bended knee to the politicians who control the regulators, with a brown envelope on a silver tray, simply in order to be able to operate. Yet many still believe it to be in their best interests for the UK to remain in the EU. They will become the playthings of politicians, as their counterparts are, and always have been, on the continent. Euro-politicians will decide which will succeed. Berlusconi, richest man in Italy, had to become a politician himself, because that is where the power lies. If he hadn't, he said, his enemies would have ruined him.

Transport of Forces - use of Europe's high speed rail network. Requisition ships under EU flag. EJIC=EU Joint Intelligence Committee under EU Security Minister.

Defence Agency: strong, single European: "buy European first', safe - guards procurement Trirectoire: BASystems, EADS and Thales as prime contractors. Defence spend 2% GDP per annum by all EU member states.

3 - Tiers of Capability:
First Tier: Britain, France, Germany—national armed forces for ESS (European Security Strategy missions).
Second Tier: Netherlands, Italy, Spain, Poland=2nd Tier capability, with lower numbers of stabilisation and peacekeeping forces. Special police forces for transition from combat to peacemaking and policing.
Third Tier: niche forces to be provided by other EU states. Specialisation in lower to medium intensity operations e.g robust peace-keeping.

USA: will remain EU's main 'strategic' partner with NATO remaining guardian of military link with American forces. Other Strategic Partners: Russia is vital for strategic ESDP: European Security. ESDP and Defence Policy, also Canada, China, India, Japan, Ukraine. Strong regional part - nerships are essential, with influence in Americas, Middle East and Africa.

Future Agenda: Role of Anglo-French Nuclear Forces to be formalised. Germany not permitted nuclear arms.

Nuclear War: EU Military strategists define the EU Defence Strategy, initiated by Berlin, and are considering a *pre-emptive nuclear first strike* – specifically envisioning the possible conduct of preventive wars. *A recent "European Defence Paper" included nuclear arms in the first strike strategy of the EU. It states that British and French nuclear powers could* *be included "explicitly or implicitly" in this preventive military option.* The authors of the study, a group of high-ranking military advisors demand energetic, prompt and inclusive armament by the EU. The goal is to reach the status of a world power able to conduct preventive wars.

But Germany has been excluded from the nuclear field. Her way round, as usual, is to use others' strength under her command. The danger is clear. *To allow Germany control over nuclear weapons is tantamount to inviting her to use them first as pressure or blackmail,* and then with the excuse of 'preventive strikes', especially with the strength of their mighty Bundeswehr, so carefully and secretly built up (on peaceful missions with NATO obligated).

The proposed European standing Army will be under German com-mand.

Germany announces that the French have agreed full cooperation. But many European nations have expressed anxiety over such proposals. The French and British are also having second thoughts. Hence Sarkozy's unusually warm friendly gesture (BBC News 27.3.2008): "I have never reduced France's European policies simply to our relations with the Germans. The Paris-Berlin axis is at the essence, but it is not enough, and I have never ceased wanting to work in close cooperation with London". This at a time when *Germany is seeking a nuclear first strike capability for NATO, which she now dominates. So France obviously wants alliance with Britain to offset the increasing belligerence of Germany, seeking total mastery of EU military affairs, within her own hidden schemes for world domination.*

The threat of total World War, with so many countries developing nuclear weapons (including Iran, N.Korea, Libya, as well as all the great Powers), makes not only for great care and deliberation, but also for world conference on how to obviate the danger of plunging the world into the greatest despoliation of mankind beyond comprehension.

DVD: Deutsche Verteidigung's Dienst::German post-war Defence Agency's Abwehr-linked Intelligence continuum of the Nazi international, originally established by the Nazi Abwehr at the German Geopolitical Centre Madrid in 1943, to keep the Nazi strategy continuing as planned.

Regionalisation owes its origin to the German concept of ethnic groups (Volksgruppen). They attach major importance to Volk (folk)=homogenous population of common blood origin and common language (as large-ly featured in Wagner's operas), Hitler and the Nazis considered that Volk live ideally as a blood community in a separate homeland – *"In der Heimat"* – on their own soil – an idyllic impossible concept in our interwoven world – ever since the tower of Babel split the peoples with a variety of tongues. They considered that Germany was the only complete state in Europe with all contained in one pure Volk. Whereas all others like England and France were a total mixture needing to be split into many region, a somewhat comic opera, of mixed paternity.

Bernard Connolly in "The Rotten Heart of Europe" and "Dirty War of Europe's Money" said: "The double-talk of politicians, bankers and bureaucrats is forcing Europe into a crippling monetary straitjacket". *The relentless, ruthless attack on national sovereignty prosecuted by the EU, described as "Coup d'état by instalments". The political collective invented by the self-serving doctrine of the 'acquis communautaire,' dictates that powers once delegated to EU remain eternal, unchallengeable. Hitler dissolved all other parties, becoming Dictator of Germany.* The blueprint is like the EEC of the Treaty of Rome, as modified by the Single European Act and the Treaty of Maastricht.

The European Court of Justice exists NOT to dispense Justice but to further the interests of the EU. In 2000 the Advocate General of the Court ruled that criticism of EU instructions was tantamount to 'blasphemy' – precipitating their planned dictatorship. All UK governments since 1970 have connived at such erosions of freedom. By supporting Britain's membership of EU Collective, they have all covertly concurred with EU's Leninist objectives. The march to monetary union threatens our prosperity, liberties and our peace. Ex-Pres. Herzog of Germany, denigrated the nation state, following Lenin in seeking their destruction. The *Maastricht Treaty, signed by P.M. John Major, deprived EU nation states of key elements of sovereignty; their currency and security transferred to a European institution for the first time – Making Britain totally subservient to EU.*

The planned future role of Germany on Leadership of EU

Bernard Connolly said the EU was only *"a cloak of German ambitions"*. It was a launch-pad for Franz Josef Strauss, 1979 Premier of Bavaria, for Germany's come-back. His primary goal was the re-establishment of the

German nation – finally wrought in 1989 with destruction of the Berlin Wall. Strauss sought ways to destroy the legend that Germany remains a country congenitally devoted to acts of aggression. But, as part of a United Europe, federal power would come before national power. So Germany would no longer be feared for her military individual strength, while she quietly, secretly and methodically rebuilt, as in 1921/2, unremarked by the rest of the World. Hence Germany concealed her real plans under the cloak of a United Europe merging the whole Continent into a *Supranational European Framework – protecting her own sovereignty whilst persuading all others to forfeit theirs*. Strauss said: "Our European attitude was the only escape hatch we had, the only approach that made a comeback possible". "I am under no illusion about the length of time it will take to set in train."

German domination has now been revealed to an astonished World, unused to such Machiavellian plans of takeover – this time without use of armed 'persuasion' – the previous German Blitzkrieg method. Under German direction the EU would evolve to a politico-military empire, a Third Great World Power, stronger than Russia or USA. *The EU, supported from incept by American industry, is actually the greatest danger to World Peace, planning greater domination from Atlantic to the Urals.* The Vatican seeks equal domination, with Germany again becoming the Holy Roman Empire. But the Vatican is left out of this equation, basically non-religious.

In fact, this now clearly German dominated EU, is becoming a reproduction of that previously planned mix of German imperialism and continental fascism, which Britain and America were compelled to defeat in two World Wars, at great sacrifice, plunging our peaceful Western World into costly chaos. Now over 60 years later, that heroic United Kingdom effectively no longer exists. *Our hitherto World famous Westminster Parliament is subordinate to the laws, decrees, instructions and regulations of the European Commission and bureaucrats in Brussels, whose enormous flow of ill-conceived instructions now simply by-pass our Parliament (often in stunned disbelief at such costly nonsense).* They upset our normally sensible balance, causing ever-increasing labour costs. Over 80% of laws, regulations, instructions flow from EU, depriving our Parliament of originating power and *turning MPs into glorified errand boys,* many no longer of any real value or purpose. Their numbers, pay and conditions should be reduced by at least 50%, unless they are inspired by their own instincts of self-preservation, to work diligently to extract

Britain from the costly embrace of GEU, and thereby restore Parliament (and themselves) to support the people they have sworn to serve.

The British Law Courts must obey the 'Superior' European Court of Justice at Strasbourg (a costly duplicate built solely to satisfy the French, who *extract 40% of EU total annual budget for their contrived CAP*). Thus it is not a Law Court in the English sense. It makes unrepealable laws for the over-swollen establishment of all EU member national states which EU conglomeration is unable to handle efficiently. As a consequence, *British people may now be extradited to any EU country, without our normal historic protection under English Laws of habeas corpus, or trial by jury.* Yet, by contrast German citizens cannot be extradited anywhere. Thus they are making European laws, but do not abide by them: further proof that the German hand is on the tiller.

In the rest of Eastern Europe, the agricultural economy has collapsed because EU prevents their exports to the West. Their media, business and agricultural land is being acquired by W. European business, mainly German. Just as planned by the Nazis, the nation states of Europe exist as self-governing entities, for whose liberty we fought two World wars, sacrificing two generations. All those nations we released from suffering under the Nazis are now in worse state under the EU net, most already back within German power.

The euro and the planned structure of the European Army are major steps in creation of that corporatist, anti-democratic, anti nation state power, based on German controlled Europe, as the *EU Constitution of a Superstate to compete against American global strength and authority.* The eternal aggression returns to the surface, now plainly seen in Germany's dominating leadership of EU. The Yugoslav War revealed to Slavs, Eastern Europeans, NATO member Greece, a totally German-dominated 'West' of aggressive embrace, they were known by the Nazis as 'subhumans'.

Yeltsin and Putin both warned that NATO expansion Eastward driven by EU, would be unacceptable to Russia. *Putin said "Our relations with the West have moved backwards since the events in the Balkans".* Russia now seeks to establish a quasi-Soviet bloc, by promoting racial and religious statelets within their former satellites, Chechnya and Georgia, and suppressing national sovereignty in an economic Supranational bloc in the East to countermand the West. *Britain has no Churchill to defend her freedom from totalitarian rule, lacking the voice of courage and faith, commitment to right and justice and freedom for all.*

Germany shows increasing power in the field of economics and finance with Germans in the major positions to influence the global economy, including bankers and financial controllers. *The German economy is now more robust than all other EU members.* They aim to establish a great German leadership role in Europe. Germany's voice has become more strident as her military and diplomatic initiatives are again strong and aggressive. *The most critical leadership roles in EU are already filled by prominent Germans, cunningly engineered to suit their desires in the Balkans, Middle East and Afghanistan, becoming a key player in EU foreign policy. All main positions in NATO are now held by Germans. The EU, now seen as GEU = German European Union, led by Germany. The planned RRF (Rapid Reaction Force), enabling Europe's collective response to crises threatening EU security, should consist of 60,000 men with 135 officers (including a strong British contingent) – under German control.* Led by Lt.General Rainer Schuwirth, ex deputy chief of NATO during the Cold War.

The European Law Enforcement Body on domestic security is headed by German Jurgen Storbeck. Combining organised crime, drug trafficking, massive immigration networks out of control, money forging and nuclear radio activity, nuclear substance trafficking, vehicle dealing, child pornography, *Germany is now creating her new role as Peacemaker in the Middle East. Joschka Fischer – ex-terrorist Marxist/Leninist extreme Left-wing, sponsored by Soviet terrorists, clique of Leninists, became Minister of Foreign Affairs under Chancellor Schröder.* Now leader of the Green Party in Germany. Kofi Annan appointed German Michael Steiner as UN special representative for Kosovo – (rewarding their crime)?

The Germans are now in top positions in economics and financial institutions, influencing global economy banks and finance:

* Horst Kohler: appointed Managing Director International Monetary Fund.

* Schreyer: "Head European Commissioner in charge of EU Budget".

* Oman Issing: One of the 6 members on the executive board of European Central Bank.

* Eberhard Uhlmann: Secretary General Management Committee European Investment Bank.

* Gerhard Cromme: Vice Chairman of Influential Round Table of Industrialists.

* Otto Lamsdorff: one of 3 Regional Chairmen of the Trilateral Commission.

* Peter Woike: ethnic German Managing Director of the World Bank, and executive Vice-President of the International Finance Corporation.
* Plus a great many bureaucrats and influential posts held by Germans. Many strongly attached to the fulfilment of Teutonic Vision of resurrection of the Holy Roman Empire.

Germany desires not only to lead, Europe, but also play a leading role generally in World affairs. She contributes troops in Afghanistan, but without undertaking action. Bodo Hombach developed a Balkan Stability Pact for Germany's peacekeeping mission in the Balkans. In September 2001 Germany took over as lead nation in the Macedonia Operation "Amber Fox", plus $140 million dollars pledged in reconstruction aid. Other countries cannot sustain such high costs. Yet in 2001 Germany was in recession with 4? million unemployed. Proving the existence of secret financial support.

In 1973 America went off the gold standard, but the dollar is now the unsecured liability of the US government, Gold is held as an insurance. *The German Central Bank holds the second largest gold reserve in the World.* Eleven EU members have signed over their national gold holdings to the European Central Bank, Frankfurt. *Britain and Canada have sold large gold holdings – bought by Germany. The operation was carried out by Gordon Brown when Chancellor, with gold at its lowest purchase level – and without explanation.* Bad smell to this deal, Brown selling off our precious gold holding at the World's lowest prices – why? In January 2007 Joschka Fischer, Minister of Foreign Affairs said "The nightmare of British euro-sceptics, the so-called Superstate – a new sovereign State to abolish the old nation states, along with their democratic government – is nothing but a synthetic construct that has nothing whatsoever to do with European reality"! – A downright lie! Seeing us as trusting sub-humans, easily befooled.

Professor Herzog said: "The nation state has ceased to exist as an impermeable structure – nor should it exist any longer". At least more honest than dissembling Fischer. British concern is for the preservation of our sovereignty and national identity of the nation state, as the only legitimate expression of the popular will. Fischer said: *"nation states will have no sovereignty once integration and federation has been completed, since federation is a traditional form towards the complete union of all nations".*

His real objective is believed to be the establishment of a Single World Communist Government, with EU a key subsidiary component. Fischer added: "The state will blame capitalism for its inability to guarantee living standards and social security. Globalisation must be organised, channelled and used as means of rescuing totalitarian control in all spheres of human society. At special times in history, violence is needed to change society". There speaks the real communist, unchanged and still seeking world globalisation/dictatorship.

Volteface: Fischer now promotes himself as Europe's Peace-maker. He persuaded Schröder to refuse to participate in any military operation in Iraq. Schröder made Fischer Germany's new representative to the European convention, drafting the Constitution. Fischer is tantamount Father of the Convention, requiring a constitutional refoundation of Europe, to enable the enlarged EU to function properly. Thus Europe is now led by a confessed Communist Fischer.

Jurgan Storbeck is the German Head of the new European police force. Modern Germany sits in a seat of power and increasing political influence in Europe and on the World scene. The EU places Security and Defence high on its political agenda, demanding its own Army as ecological further step towards integration.

U.S.A.

John McCloy, US Occupation Chief, returned to America in 1952 saying "mission accomplished". *He used Rockefeller funds from CFR to support the return of Nazis.* His departure marked a new phase in post-war Germany, now self-governed, without interference from occupying powers. McCloy became consultant for Rockefeller, with close ties with *CIA and Council of Foreign Relations (CFR) who supported Germany.* In 1953, McCloy became Chairman of Rockefeller's organisation helping Germany and other schemes.

Harry Truman, menswear retailer, became President of the USA after the sudden death of Roosevelt, and was thrown, poorly briefed, into handling both German and Japanese surrenders. He discovered the intricate plotting. Edwin Pauly was spy for Dulles brothers, helped them shift Nazi assets out of Europe. Then became supporter of Nixon, part of the same group. George Bush leased oil rigs to Pauly as his best customer, fiddling together. James S. Martin's book, "All Honourable Men" states *"We were stopped from denazification, hunting down criminals, by American business. The bigger operators arrange the World affairs"*, meaning the Rockefeller Group. Roosevelt was aware of this and other plots and acted accordingly to frustrate them, knowing how industrialists cover up their crimes. However, he died too soon, and his plan to bring Nazi supporters to justice, died with him.

The *British American Canadian Corporation* became World Commerce Corporation in 1947. Liquidated in 1962 for tax reasons. Purpose was restoration of economic balance in Europe. *Re-building Germany in direct violation of Roosevelt's clear instructions.* Members, all with British/American Intelligence and OSS, included Charles Hambro, David Ogilvy, Nelson Rockefeller, John McCloy, Victor Sassoon, Frank Ryan. *Thus these British and Americans never intended to destroy Nazi Germany. The OSS recruited Wall Street and industry leaders to reduce the cost of rebuilding Germany post war, all helping to finance Germany's amazingly quick recovery.* Bormann also drew up an elaborate plan for their comeback, supported by Hitler, hiding huge capital assets to regain strength. *"Action Fatherland"* was created by German corporations in foreign countries with Nazi agents and with the help of the American Republican Party.

McCloy was funded by well-known fascists, seeking to sabotage the "denazification programme". Heads of the Army of Occupation and Military Government were filled with American business leaders with Nazi ties. Dismantling I.G. Farben was stopped. John McCloy set free war criminals. Wall Street firms were the centre of the sabotage of denazification. Brown Bros & Harriman, Dillon & Reed, Sullivan and Sullivan & Cromwell. Leaders of this corruption included *Prescott Bush, John and Alan Dulles.* Nazi tarning (hiding looted treasure), was their best way back to power, with financial aid from American supporters. *The Group's next plan was to provoke the Cold War of US versus Soviet.* Joe McCarthy created the fever of "hunting the Reds". *J.F. Dulles helped start the Korean War. 10 years after Prescott Bush had his companies seized for trading with the enemy, he was elected to Congress, choosing Richard Nixon as Vice-President Candidate in 1952,* after Nixon agreed with Alan Dulles to hide evidence of his treason, from Nazi documents. *So New York Banks which had funded Hitler, now funded Nixon.*

The CFR (Council on Foreign Relations), the *Trilateral Union* (founded by Rockefeller) formed a *conspiracy of ideas, an ideological battle of modern elements of illuminati.* They believe in globalism, *seeking world government.* CFR, established 1921 with the help of the Rockefeller Foundation. Seeking to influence world affairs they *helped finance Hitler from their CFR Study Group.* In 1946/7 they influenced President Truman's decision to help reconstruct war-ravaged Europe with American financial aid, known as the Marshall Plan. *Rockefellers had Germano/Turkish roots, and favoured Germany with strong financial backing.* David Rockefeller was helped by the Rothschilds to develop his massive fortune, including ownership of the *Chase Manhattan Bank (now J.P.Morgan Chase). Chairman of CFR 1970-1985,* he formed close relations with all leading statesmen, from Harry S Truman to modern times. After the merger, his International Council included Henry Kissinger, Lee Kuan Yew and George Schultz, the current chairman, dealing with General Electric, Standard Oil etc. *The new International Advisory Committee included Gianni Agnelli, John Loudon (Chairman Royal Dutch Shell) and Henry Ford III. Schultz picked the Bush team, known as the Vulcans, led by Condoleezza Rice, with Dick Cheney, George P. Schultz and Colin Powell.* They were a secret cabal of internationalists around the *Rockefeller family,* conspiring with others around the world to build more integrated, global political and economic structure as *'One World'.* (cf Rockefeller's Memoirs and You Tube History Channel documentary re Rockefeller family.)

The World Bank (connected with Chase Bank) Presidents John McCloy, Eugene Black Sr, George Woods and James Wolfenden, also Director Rockefeller Foundation. Very powerful organisation, with Kissinger. *In 1965 Rockefeller founded the "Council of the Americas"* to stimulate economic integration, playing a *key role in establishing North America Free Trade Agreement (NAFTA) in 1992, including Bill Clinton. A conspiracy to form the North American Union-a globalist plan to develop American/Canadian/ Mexican alliance similar to EU, to further World Government.*

Rockefeller wrote: "The world is now more sophisticated and prepared to march towards a World Government which will never again know war, but only peaceful prosperity for the whole world of humanity. *The supra - national sovereignty of an intellectual elite and world bankers is surely preferable to the national auto-determination practised in the past cen - turies.* It is also our duty to inform the Press of our convictions as to the historic future of the century. *Including CFR, David Rockefeller, IMF, World Bank". There we have the picture summed up in his own words as to why we should all accept his wealth-inspired wisdom and World Organisation under the control of plutocrats, whose money, they believe, entitles them to rule the world.* It is due to their misguided handling of affairs that we experience the present world situation and our present problem with their connived at GEU (German dream of control of all Europe), to the detriment of Britain. *They call themselves The Elite.*

The Elite: *David Rockefeller founded the Trilateral Commission in 1973 with Zbigniew Brzezinski, who idealised Karl Marx theories on world-order politics and followed them closely* (cf his book Between Two Ages). *The 3 sides were US and Canada, Europe and Japan.* These included 325 distinguished citizens devoted to One World Government. TC goals were close Trilateral cooperation in keeping the peace. The creation of a community of the developed nations to address the larger concerns confronting mankind. *Ted Heath was a member. Frances Maude is a member. Brzezinski was a classic CFR man – a globalist leaning towards communism, declaring National Sovereignty no longer a viable concept.* Marxism represents a further vital and creative stage in the maturing of man's wisdom; Marxism is the victory of the external active man over the inner passive man; the *victory of reason over belief.* Hence the direction of *the CFR, who regarded themselves as the world's elite. Leaders in business, industry, banking, government and mass media in N. America, West Europe and Japan viewed themselves as World Leaders moving towards a communist style dictatorship of the Elite.* Private multinational Banks, including Chase Manhattan, loaned $52 Billion dollars to developing countries, overhauling IMF (International Monetary Fund), another source of credit. *Their intention was to be the vehicle for multinational consolidation of the commercial and banking interests, by seizing control of the political government of the US.*

Jimmy Carter, founder member Trilateralist was made President US with the influence of CFR and Trilateralists. He became a Candidate overnight, like Eisenhower. *The Elite can make or break any Candidate they choose for President* (and no doubt have sway in our politics, for *money speaks all languages*). Membership: present and past Presidents, Ambassadors, Secretaries of State, Wall St. investors, International Bankers, University Presidents, Selected Senators, Ministers, wealthy entrepreneurs meet at annual secret meetings with very select guests. *Elite formation: Centre:* made up of the *Czar and members of the Inner Circle,* who are the decision makers, totally informed and involved in the Global Union movement *led by David Rockefeller.* Then come Inner Ring, Centre Ring and Outer Ring. Reminds one of *similarity with the illuminati, who started it all with Adam Weishaupt (ex Jesuit) and worship of the devil (the Angel of Light).*

Federal Reserve Directors: Study of Corporate Banking Influence (1976) Chart reveals the *linear connection between the Rothschilds and the Bank of England, and the London banking houses which ultimately control the Federal Reserve Banks.* The two principal Rothschilds' representatives in New York are JP Morgan Co., and Kuhn Loeb & Co which set up the Jekyll Island Conference at which the Federal Reserve Act was drafted, directing the successful campaign to have the *plan enacted into law by Congress,* and purchasing the controlling amounts of stock in the Federal Reserve Bank of New York in 1914. This same family has retained control ever since. *A most audacious seizure of American currency by tricking the government.*

Every Republican President and Vice-President since Eisenhower (suspiciously sudden promotion from Colonel to General, to be awarded the position of Senior Commander in Chief on Invasion, Combined Forces Europe (still apparently acting on orders or instructions received from above) with the exception of Agnew and Cheney, had either direct ties to aiding the Nazis and war criminals, or strong family relations with Nazis, revealing the strong pro-German element in USA.

The Cold War dragged on, reaching its peak in 1960, with the threat of nuclear war during the Cuban Missile Crisis. *President John F. Kennedy chose détente with Kruschev, thus ending the Cold War, but sealing his own death by assassins.* The Nazis were fermenting the Cold War, but overplayed their hand with over-much communism hysteria, when the American fear of communist Russia had already subsided. *The development of EU with its move towards a similar form of dictatorship, and Germany's close relationship with Russia, now revealed the Nazi ploy of the threat of World communism to be the usual German use of cunning deceit, to create fear of a phantom enemy, to gain their ends with full support of "useful idiots.*

Soviet Russia's Planned EU

Vladimir Bukovsky (Soviet dissident) warns: "A Dictatorship in No time."

In 1971 he exposed the psychiatric abuse of political prisoners in USSR, after 12 years imprisonment in Soviet jails, labour camps and psychiatric institutions. Finally expelled in 1976 in exchange. Testified in 1992 at trial against Communist Party of Soviet Union. *Yeltsin later gave him access to top secret documents of Politburo, planning future structure of the European Union to become a totalitarian regime, similar to former USSR.*

Together the Soviets and Leftwing Europe would hijack the European project, turning it into a Federal State, citing the *1989 meeting of Gobachëv and Trilateral Commission delegates. Valery Giscard d'Estaing said: "a new modern federal state would emerge in Western Europe".* 13 years later Giscard authored the EU Constitution. He said, "Western Europe is experiencing a 'perestroika', changing its structures". *Revealing EU plans to absorb East European states, once satellites of the Soviet regime; now to be ensnared by another future dictatorship.*

Armaments Business: Moscow is seen in Berlin as unrivalled partner, with joint ventures in aluminium, steel, aeronautic and space industries e,g EADS and Russian aeronautic and space industry, as joint armaments business, with cooperation in military operations in third states. The Germans use Antonov Russian wide-body transport, costing many million euros. Germany and EU are particularly affected by the rise in OPEC oil power, since USA and China have already secured a large part of the present increase. USA, meantime, buying up Libya and Norway oil. Their strategy: aim to secure Germany's energy supply by end of 2007, against growing world-wide energy demands. Problem: rivalry between resources-rich states of Sudan, Congo and Middle East.

Whenever Germany sought to extend her Reich, she always first diplomatically removed any possible Russian threat, aware that friendship with Russia is in her best strategic interest. Schroeder and Putin signed agreements to "establish strategic partnerships in every sphere", with joint high technology cooperation, including piping natural gas through the Baltic Sea directly into West Europe. *Russia is the largest single partner of EU and the largest supplier of uranium. The Asia Times says the Russian economic future lies with Europe and China.* Germany is the biggest investor in Russia There is no natural geographic barrier north of the Carpathian Mountains to act as buffer between newly resurgent Russia and the ambitious German-led EU. So, in 2007 Germany signed a joint agreement with Putin to protect Germany's East flank. *The EU now seeks a separate pact with Russia, growing ever closer to the communist regime in its Left inclination.*

The core issue of the 21st century is clearly the *balance of power in Europe,* with USA being pushed out of the equation and no longer underwriting European security. *The current leadership is principally between Merkel and Putin.* Germany seeks to secure her weak eastern border with Russian Treaties, to maintain the balance of power. In 1995, Bukovsky published *"EUSSR", clarifying "Soviet Roots of European Integration",* as the plan of Gobachëv, Italian Communists and German Social Democrats to combat capitalism and *hijack EU into a federal state.* Bukovsky said the original idea, after Soviet break-up, was for "convergency" i.e. Soviet Union to become more socialist. Then both structures to converge into the new Soviet structure. Those governing Europe to stabilise East Europe, participating in the political reorganisation of the World. EU to extend beyond the Balkans, creating a Black Sea dimension. The European Army to confront any disruptions to EU expansion.

Moscow urging Euro-Asian alliance. Russian ties to N.E. Asia reach to Vladivostock, and border on China, Korea and India (indirectly). A geographical triangle is now forming in Russia's Asian region, with Russia as mediator bridging the Atlantic and Pacific nations. Germany in 2006 sought a strategic partnership with Moscow for energy resources to be reserved long-term for the German economy, especially natural gas and oil. *Giving visions of a Germano-Slav domination with a G/R merger?*

The European Superstate will be offset in Asia by the emerging massive power bloc of greater Asia, S.E.Asia and the Indian sub-continent. Meanwhile competition grows for African resources. Competition between Latin America and the Caribbean continues between leading nation power blocs: Germany, Russia, China. *The oil-rich Middle East is wooed by all until overshadowed by the Islamist threat, rousing now militarised Europe to deal with the challenge. The rising Fourth Reich plans to place Jerusalem at the heart of the EU power bloc – with support of the Vatican. But this could become the catalyst to unleash future events in the form of one more German Russian treaty before WWIII.*

90% of Albanians want independence. Belgrade wants to keep its sov -

ereignty over Kosovo, but EU and US support the UN plan to give Kosovo internationally supervised independence, with EU holding the key role. Russia rejected the new Con/Treaty draft, whilst jockeying with Germany for power in Europe. Germany wants Kosovo as symbol of its uncontested leadership of Europe – as a sign of Berlin's reach and influence over the entire continent of Europe, from the North Sea to the Mediterranean, including the crucial crossroads of the Balkan Peninsula (see map). Think-tank Stratfor indicated German interest in Kosovo: *Merkel said bluntly at G8 summit (with Putin present), that Kosovo will be independent,* echoed by Bush and UK. Stratfor commented *"Merkel is seeking to help Germany emerge as the major European power, and what better way than to force Russia publicly into confrontation – and then make her retreat* (but she may live to regret taking on Putin as adversary)".

History

EU says learning history is of little or no value; so cease teaching it in schools. But history may be turned in its course by great events or individuals. 'The knowledge of history is the beginning of wisdom', and fosters the ability to weigh situations accurately. George Washington created historic greatness in founding America. Lincoln's Gettysburg address made World-famous history in one line: "Government of the people, by the people, for the people", leaving its mark and influence on World history.

Biographer William Manchester said: "Churchill saved Western civilisation". H.S. Commager wrote the Introduction of Churchill's biography of his ancestor Marlborough: "Churchill's reading of history made him exalt heroic virtue. He was Roman rather than Greek, admiring Roman virtues of order, justice, fortitude, resoluteness, magnanimity, as British virtues". Churchill said: "as a law of history, a people who flout these virtues is doomed to decay and dissolution – a people who respects them will prosper and survive". Our nation lives today because great leaders of the past learned and practised heroic virtues.

British school children now have a woeful ignorance of history. Who is to save us now from WWIII? Churchill in his "History of the Second World War" wrote: "In War, Resolution, in Defeat, Defiance. In Victory, Magnanimity, in Peace: Goodwill". For him, History was a moral scripture, authorative, straight forward, simple. A struggle between the forces of right and wrong, freedom and tyranny, the future and the past: *"This island race was on the side of right, progress and enlightenment". "History teaches lessons from the past to apply to the present."* The contemplation of past ages endured and survived by mankind, provides patience and courage; that posterity had given a nation 'its finest hour' encouraged resolution, strengthening the ability to confront crises that seemed insurmountable.

History follows great cycles, the same themes recurring again and again, playing out the same drama from age to age, surviving the vicissitudes of the past. Giving hope that we might survive those of present and future. *Four times Britain fought to rescue Europe from the grip of a tyrant: Louix XIV, Napoleon, Kaiser Wilhelm and Hitler* – succeeding in saving Europe and the cause of liberty and justice: a recurring pattern, auguring well for the future of 'this island race' and the welfare of mankind. *History bears witness to the vital importance of national character,* as important to a people as to an individual. "Battles are the principal milestones in secular history. All great struggles of history have been won by superior willpower, wresting victory in the teeth of heaviest odds. The story of the human race is War" – cf. Marlborough, Chatham, Wolfe, Clive, Washington, Lee: great war leaders with the vital importance of leadership. Nelson was outnumbered and outgunned, yet he resolutely planned his attack, bringing his own death, fearlessly, with ultimate victory for the British Empire, which he loved dearly and served bravely.

History, well taught, inspires our children to broader horizons and best use of their ability. But *EU insists (with German approval), that history teaching in our schools must now begin from 1945, for obvious reasons of discounting Britain's victorious past, blocking their efforts to reduce her to a Third World status.* Growing numbers of children avoid schools and roam the streets, often in gangs, committing robbery and burglary, using guns and knives. Children now murder both children and adults. In many areas they are seemingly out of control by police and local authorities. There are *insufficient police* to carry out their manifold duties. *They too suffer under ever increasing and conflicting EU regulations and instructions under which they are bound.* Just as people in general are unknowingly trapped in ignorance and bewilderment at the continuous, almost daily increase of conflicting EU regulations. *Freedom is become a wishful fantasy. We have mastered nature and gained our freedom, but have rejected the limitations of the human condition.* We are now witnessing a general revolt against civilisation and a desire to embrace a life of perpetual irresponsibility and self-indulgence. *Beware of these so-called modernists who seek to strike out our past history and ancient, ethical values.* They skillfully and consistently lead us to corruption of proven good, in place of our age-old proven mores. They misguide our leaders and seek to corrupt our youth, to satisfy their own demonic lifestyle and twisted perversions.

We dare not continue to turn away, and pretend not to notice what we know to be the evil *perversion and corruption of our family life,* and the upbringing of our children. For the sake of their future and that of our country, and all that we hold dear-and have fought for valiantly in the past, we must now have the courage to stand up and be counted against these evils, before they succeed in destroying all that we hold good. *The tenets of our universal faith are bound simply and clearly, today as ever, in those God-given 10 Commandments.* They must still be the unquestioned basic guide of our teachers, leaders in religion and government, legislative and administrative.

So many of our elected leaders seem so quickly to forget the duty they owe to the people who elect them, with their promise to put the people and their country above all else. Instead some seek their own self-promotion, selling us out to the insidious foreign influence of those who seek to demean us into a vassal state, losing all that we have built up, and defended literally and faithfully all our lives. Churchill, and our courageous, worthy leaders of our long history, have led us fearlessly and righteously, upholding our rights as a free, sovereign nation. *Beware now the enemy within,* seeking to rob us and deprive our children of our ancient rights to conduct our lives in the freedom of our beloved Country. *Let them now return to those tenets which made Britain admired and respected throughout the world.*

History of over 2,000 years made the British Empire the greatest ever known. This island earned its world renown by the strength, intelligence and fortitude of its people who, ever willingly, fought for their rights and freedom. Our children should be taught the value of Freedom and Sovereignty gained by the efforts of their forbears, who were proud to defend 'King and Country' and their fellow Englishmen and women. Now is once again time to uphold those strong talents against the GEU's efforts to reduce us to pawns in their communist-style dictatorship of this proposed Superstate. There is a map produced by the EU to effectively allotting major parts of Britain to France, Scandinavia and Germany, with *total removal of the name of ENGLAND, leaving a stub of an island about the size of Jersey.*

Common Purpose: a registered Charity, *supposedly an innocuous local organisation of leadership studies.* In fact, used primarily for *networking for EU for leaders primarily within the public sector.* Government departments have paid substantial sums to CP for staff instruction (indoctrination?). The Department for Work and Pensions paid £238,000 from 2003 to 2007 to procure management training in leadership for senior managers, to 'enhance capability as potential leaders'. A spokeswoman said: "In pursuit of our charitable objects we run educational programmes for leaders and decision-makers across all sectors and every stage of career". One third from the public sector, and the remainder from private and voluntary sectors. They claim 25,000 members, dedicated to their teaching. *In fact implementing EUs instructions on corruption, feeding some 100,000 'useful idiots' from its gravy train. They have already penetrated BBC (with some 400 controlling news and current affairs), newspapers, council executives, Church of England, NHS (cunningly destroyed from within over 20 years).* CP members control Quangos' budget of about £124 billion, and NHS budget of £90 billion, about £210 billion or one third of our taxes.

Global Analyst states that the British 'Fabian' Government (New Labour) is cover for a 'gradualist' revolution, under the leadership of John Prescott as Deputy PM, former ship's steward, long-term Bolshevik, with a long catalogue of botches, failures, aborted schemes and fiascos, His Head of Personnel Selection is *Julia Middleton, who runs CP as Founder and Chief Executive of a vast networking organisation CP is used continuously on the European Union Collective, but never defined. It is, in fact, a subversive organisation of Neurological Linguistic Control, specialising in mind control and brainwashing.* Expert psychological manipulative techniques are used by corrupt intelligence agencies. Similar to the old Moral Rearmament, stripping all loyalties by the established neuro-control technique, by persuading subjects to confess all past sins. These then used as blackmail to lead to the next step,-demands for money, depriving the victims of their independence and chaining them permanently to the set-up. The standard Tavistock-originated cult and indoctrination technique.

When *Julia Middleton set up Common Purpose in 1988,* as Chief Executive, she stated that *their aims were to improve the way society works, by increasing the number of informed individuals actively engaged in shaping the future of the area in which they live and work.* By bringing leaders from diverse backgrounds together, CP creates new networks for current and future decision makers. They claim to have developed programmes world-wide through Common Purpose International, from Sweden to S. Africa, to India. Julia Middleton is also on the Investors for Diversity, National Centre for Diversity, an independent org. with a National Advisory Board.

CP sweeps away all notions resident in victim's mind and psyche, to be replaced by 'slides', or politically correct notions imposed by control manipulators:
1 - A predetermined 'consensus line is promulgated before the group.

2 - Notions which conflict are then dismissed and rudely debunked. Any dissension sharply made to look foolish.

3 - 'Lines' unveiled to be accepted without question - 'preconceived' 'slides'. So reasonable that nobody would dare object to them. But a large vocabulary of pejorative epithets would be directed at non-conformers. These are all carefully conceived objectives from the powers behind GEU to cause mental problems generally, from school age into adulthood, concentrating attention on personal enjoyment with drink, drugs, loud music, singing and dancing, watching sport rather than taking part in venturesome activity, making heroes of those who strut their images on stage and screen. Their object being to keep everybody's attention away from politics and the evil plot secretly engineered to rob us of our rights of Freedom and Sovereignty and plunge us all into the Soviet style dictatorship, so cunningly being 'unknowingly', prepared for us by those who believe themselves destined to rule the world.

Angela Merkel & Her Con/Treaty

Born Hamburg 1954, educated in the German Democratic Republic of Russian communist controlled zone, as scientist. Won the Election of 2005, becoming the first woman Chancellor (=PM) as Protestant leader of CDU (Catholic male-dominated Party, Christian Democratic Union). Often compared with Margaret Thatcher as Iron Lady.

Fully supportive of the EU under German command, Merkel was deter -

mined to force through the EU Constitution despite France and the Netherlands decisively voting down the Referendum, to the plotters' dismay. With the aid of Bertelsmann Group meetings of leading European statesmen, Merkel arrived at a dishonest piece of trickery. *By exchanging the properly named Constitution for Treaty, with a few minuscule changes, she demanded that all members sign in December 2007, this Con/Treaty* (as I name it, for a 'con' it assuredly is), *without permitting a referendum. Thus tricking the people of Europe into its acceptance without explanation or vote for or against this new Superstate dictatorship – keeping them in ignorance of the plot.* Obviously anticipating they would vote it down on learning the truth. Merkel's Diktat was accepted en bloc by ALL Heads of Government, scared of this Iron Frau.

Merkel's motive is simply Power for Germany, in complete control of both Germany and Europe, using the EU as a tool. She used the old German aggression tactics of threatened compulsion, to force acquiescence from the Polish delegation, solely daring to criticise. The Czech delegation called that Brussels summit a fiasco, confirming the fears of their Leader Vaclav Klaus.

So *Merkel has emerged as the centre point of European affairs, with Germany as core European Power, dominating the Continent and reducing her neighbours to powerlessness – until they toe the line as obedient allies. Imperial Germany played a similar dominating role, from its rise in 1870 to its fall in WWI.* Merkel is now rising rapidly in power, busily engaged in bringing Europe together exactly as she plans. "United under Germany" means a Supernationalist State, primarily serving Germany's interests. Hugo Chavez, President of Venizuela has compared her CDU Party to Hitler's Nazi Party *"the same right wing that supported Hitler and fascism"*. But the GEUs real direction is Left Wing (as her background), communist style dictatorship.

On 23rd June 2007 Karel de Gucht, Belgian Foreign Minister said "The aim of the Constitution was to be more readable; the aim of this Treaty is to be unreadable and unclear". It is a success!

In motivating WWI Germany goaded Austria and Hungary into increasing their demands on Serbia, beyond her capacity to meet. This led to war with Germany trying to resurrect the Holy Roman Empire. Recently Germany again put Serbia into a difficult situation, by personally *acknowledging the separation of Croatia and Slovenia from Yugoslav federation in 1991, with support of the Vatican. So Catholic Croatia and Slovenia have become EU colonies under German protection, just as in the War as Hitler's allies.*

18th October 2007 at Lisbon, the European Council passed the German: "EU Reform Treaty", replacing the original "EU Constitution" with a Federal State. Labour MPs protested at their own Ministers' acceptance of EU policies, creating the scandal of our Foreign Minister David Miliband seeking ratification without referendum, keeping the British people in ignorance of such connivance, fearing their wrath, once this evil plotting were revealed.

The EU has become the major single economic and trade bloc, but not yet matched by military strength except the powerful German Bundeswehr. But Church and State now co-operating as with Charlemagne. Merkel their Führer, with troops in Afghanistan (but NOT fighting), Balkans, Sudan, Horn of Africa, Southern Caucasus and Palestinian territories. *Now claiming the right to nuclear weapons as a major deterrent, although forbidden by the Allies.* Her aggressive tone matches Germany's strong economy – demanding a more stream-lined Europe, accepting Germany as EU's real political economic and military strength.

Merkel now seeks a new Partnership and Co-operation Agreement between EU and Russia on Baltic States, missile defence, political devel-opments in Kosovo, Palestine, Lebanon, Afghanistan, Sudan, Iran: all need to be settled, with a long list of economic and political problems.

France still furnishes Libya with nuclear equipment and armaments, and claims influence in North Africa and the Mediterranean nations. Germany calls this "irresponsible national single-handiness" (exactly like Germany), saying: "In EU each country cannot do as it pleases" (always excepting Germany). President Sarkozy thinks control of the South East coast of neighbouring North Africa and Mid-Eastern states, gives Berlin the opportunity to extend her influence southward to include resources-rich Algeria and Libya. But France prevails in the Middle East. Libya chose France as strategic partner, and France supplied Libya with atomic energy plant and a major weapons deal with EADS, storing up future trouble.

The dispatch of a German submarine, in September 2007, to the port of Algiers, underscores the German military strength in Algeria (contesting the French hold) – thus Germany horning in on the French territory. Germany trains Algerian soldiers in Germany (Germanisation process), seeking take-over of Algeria, a North African country incorporated into NATO through anti-terror measures. (German crafty guile, using 'terrorism threat' as excuse). Now supplies Algeria with arms, soon to be sealed in a treaty. What will be the French reaction? Algeria has waged war over Islamist rebels for the past 15 years. Now Police and Intelligence services of both countries are co-operating, with accord, in the War on Terror.

The Con/Treaty will have a President and Foreign Minister, and have the right to sign treaties on our behalf, as a single legal personality. Under the Charter of Fundamental Rights, EU judges will decide more of our laws, including asylum, criminal justice and policing, drastically reducing our English laws. National vetoes were all dropped after a short debate – so *no opposition was permitted.*

The Maastricht Treaty of 1992, established a common European citizen-ship. A Sovereign of any member state automatically became a European citizen, and vassal to the federal government of EU, subject to their court's judgements, with no right of appeal – including Queen Elizabeth II as Mrs Windsor. However, we claim the legitimacy of many foundation laws, like The Act of Settlement, Corporation Oaths Act, Crown in Parliament Act, The Act of Union and Royal Marriage Act and Succession of Throne Act of Settlement of 1701.

In 2007 Merkel demanded that the National Armed Forces of all member states be combined into a single Armed Force, led by Germany. All arranged by decree of the executive, without the slightest democratic feedback: Dictatorship in full swing! *The EU Strategy Group* (top ranks of 21 states), seeking the strategic reorientation of the EU, *agreed the merging of European national forces into one unified EU Army – under German command.* ESG has a special role designing the EU future, using threat of impending war(?) to force through Eastern expansion of EU against any resistance. (Surely Britain would rebuff such bullying?) We would lose our own defence capacity, threatened already with many overseas commitments.

Wolfgang Schauble, previous Minister of the Interior, declared: "Germany might be required or compelled by its own security considerations, to achieve the stabilisation of Eastern Europe alone, *and in traditional manner". (The old German 'persuasion' by aggressive threat of military force – hence the importance of keeping Britain independent).*

In 2006 Bernd Neumann, Berlin State Culture Minister said: "The medieval Europe-wide German Reich is a valid model for the union of European countries today into a Superstate". The memory of the Holy Roman Empire of the German nation, reveals an inner historical consistency with the founding and steady expansion of EU. A European Army is needed now to confront disruptions to EU expansion plans – to cooperate with NATO and UN. But Germans are already now heading NATO and UN. So this is clearly a German enterprise, building her own mighty Armed Forces, whilst arranging all others to combine into EU Armed Forces, under German full control.

September 2007: Merkel and Foreign Minister F.W. Steinmeier said: "Reforming EU Treaties does not solve all EU's real problems. *A Common Energy Policy is needed* to meet the challenge of the climate change; the need to overhaul and reshape the World's energy system (especially Germany's), which now relies upon imported oil and gas. *A new Partnership and Cooperation Agreement is needed between EU and Russia"*. The Russo-German Pact main point: no natural barrier exists north of the Carpathian Mountains as buffer to protect Germany's eastern borders (her weak spot), to maintain the balance of power with Putin's resurging Russia. Hence her urgent desire for joint protection pact with Putin – as before with Stalin.

Early 2008 Merkel demanded that Poland rescind 1945 post-war decrees expelling Germans from Danzig, Pomerania, Silesia and East Prussia, and expulsion from Czech land taken over by Hitler. She said that all Germans from the East must be accorded the right to their homeland (surely Germany), deprived when expelled after 1945 Allied Victory, forcing Germany to return all stolen land and goods. The German leaders use EU to pursue their own ends and overturn the rightful decrees of Allied Victory in the second German war. *They persist until they have won back all previous Nazi forced and stolen gains.*

The GEU Reform Treaty: Merkel Mandate for Eurostate

Since the Treaty of Rome and the European Committee Act 1972, Britain ceased to be a legally independent nation. Majority voting automatically applies to Crown Courts, Parliament and people "without further enactment". (Clause 2.1 ECA 1972). Successive Treaties have extended the powers of the original Treaty. Now a larger Treaty is signed at Lisbon, with text by the German Foreign Office, plus EU Parliament and Commission, on 18th October 2007. Merkel demanded that all Heads of State and Representatives sign without argument, though *admitting it to be well nigh the same as the original.*

This Lisbon Treaty is the constitutional culmination of the federalist project, which has been the political dynamic of European integration since the Schuman Declaration of 1950 proclaimed the European Coal and Steel Community to be "the first step in the federation of Europe". Commemorated 9th May each year as Europe Day. In 2004 Belgian Prime Minister Guy Verhofstadt proclaimed the EU Constitution to be "the capstone of a European Federal State".

The Lisbon Treaty makes a few minor alterations. But the legal-political effect is the same, giving it supremacy over the British Constitution and all others. *It has the constitutional form of a supranational European Federation – in effect a Superstate, with full legal personality, separate from and superior to its Member States.* Thus able to sign Treaties in all areas, with its own President, High Representative (=Foreign Minister) diplomatic service, embassies, Public Prosecutor and law-making powers.

It gives the new Union a *unified constitutional structure, bringing all areas of government within its aegis* (Art.4 Teu and 1-6 Feu). *Blair accepted it as a mandate from the European Council, and signed without question or discussion with Parliament or colleagues.* He then simply stated this fact in Parliament without explanation, and immediately resigned as Prime Minister, to the applause of fellow MPs whom he had just agreed to disempower permanently from control of most of this nation's life. A trickster to the end, betraying his country's freedom and wittingly forcing us into subservience. A farewell that will be recorded in Britain's history to his discredit.

Jim Murphy, Minister for Europe, confirmed that the mandate is 'complete, closed and will not be replaced'. So Angela Merkel got her Germanic way, despite this unknown departure from practice. Her proposals are not compatible with any democratic principle. *Objections from Poland (supported by Czechoslovakia) were ruthlessly rejected,* as all other requests for democratic discussion. The democratic voices of the peoples of Europe (hitherto not permitted to be heard) must now be raised loudly, in concert, to cause this dictatorial German Con/Treaty to be rejected.

On 9th October 2007, the European Scrutiny Committee of the House of Commons published a report, concluding that the provisions of the pro - posed "Reform Treaty" were, for all practical purposes, the same as the

EU Constitution rejected in 2005 by the French and Dutch people, and upon which, almost all sitting MPs had, in their election manifestos promised their electors a Referendum. Making it crystal clear that their Con/Treaty is a blatant lie, with *EU, as is their usual practice, refusing to accept a decisive NO from the Referendum.* This dictatorial "constitutional' enforcement makes a democratic Referendum indispensable. Labour Party Committee Chairman, Michael Connarty, accused Miliband of collaboration with Germany to the detriment of British interests, and demanded a Referendum for all citizens. So many Labour politicians want us out of GEU without delay. *They know the British people would vote NO in a Referendum, without even knowing the whole truth.*

German Support for an EU Army

On 6th May 2008, Germany's Foreign Minister Steinmeier called for greater efforts to create a *common EU Army*. To be clear, ultimately this would not be a Force assembled from contingents of national armies, as with the existing Eurocorps. It would be a fully integrated EU standing army, financed and controlled by Brussels, and recruiting its personnel directly from across the EU. As with any federal army, it could be available not only for common defence against external enemies, and for projection of military power around the globe, but also for deployment anywhere within the EU in support of the civil power. Provisions in the Lisbon treaty would take the EU some steps closer to the eventual goal of a common army, arranged and commanded by Germany.

The Euro

"The euro 'on which the Sun never sets:' speaks German", says Teubert of 'German Foreign Policy'. Sphere of Influence: from the Caribbean to the Indian Ocean and the Pacific. Also in the French Depts. of South America and the Indian Ocean; Kosovo and Montenegro; French Polynesia and New Caledonian currencies, and those of 16 countries in West and Central Africa. The European Central Bank: Frankfurt's status is developed by the German Finance Ministry, with an upper limit of 3% of GNP fixed for stability. The euro determines German strength and control of Europe, enabling it to become a Superpower, uniting the European continent as the Kaiserreich planned before WWI – continuing EEC and claiming the euro would promote and support peace in Europe. *But the German people remain attached to their D-Mark, associated with their post-war economic miracle!*

Germany is already the greatest power within the EU – still growing, whilst undermining the sovereignty of other nation states, to weaken their position. Using the euro as one of the instruments of German policy, alongside German ethnic group policies and regionalisation – ending in Europe completely dominated by Germany. But the euro is generally unpopular.

Destruction of Britain's Economy by the EU

(as researched by David Noakes, editor of *Westminster News*)

Gordon Brown, when Chancellor, boasted of his "Golden Rule" – to keep public borrowing under 40% of Britain's GDP (Gross Domestic Product). On the surface, this amounted to 37.5% = £1,330 billions in 2007. But he is a wily hider of true statistics. Inflation is way beyond the quoted figure of 2.5%, factually climbing well over 6.5%. *Thus £800 billion of PFI borrowing, £700 billion of pension debt and £100 billion Northern Rock costs are simply NOT added to stated costs.* The real borrowing is ever increasing (as with hasty attempts to remedy error of 10% tax increase, needing about £3 billion to cover the forced turnaround). This Government's true borrowing must be approaching £2,000 billion, at an ever increasing interest rate. Imagine a mortgage debt at high interest rate, inexorably leading to bankruptcy.

Quangos caused this hype in expenditure. *Some 8,500 quangos now cost £167 billion per annum, about 12% of GDP,* as reported nationally in 2007. The NHS costs £90 billion, with an internal quango costing £60 billion. *In 2006 the Cabinet Office reported a quango cost of £124 billion, revealed by the Daily Telegraph. Yet 10 years ago the cost of quangos was negligible. Quangos are the brainchild of the EU as bribery to buy patronage of EU, with our money. Over 100,000 influential people are bribed with salaries of £100,000 to £300,000 to do little but smooth the way for EU – to enforce EU regulations.* As a result the Treasury is unable to pay its bills and the pound keeps falling, keeping the Bank of England on tenderhooks.

EU regulations cost Britain £100 billion per annum (7.5% of GDP) according to the 2005 Annual Report of the Government's Better Regulation Task Force. David Arculus, Managing Director, says *EU regulation is now our biggest industry.* We now bend under the weight of about 115,000 of them, ever pouring out of Brussels. According to the Treasury Pink Book, *we lose £45 billion on our foreign exchange with EU.* We were solemnly promised by Heath in 1972 that EU would be good for trade. It has been a disaster, with trade benefit going to EU.

Over £5 billion NET annual contribution is now increased by Blair's unauthorised handover of Thatcher's hard-won £3 billion rebate, to *total £8 billion.* The *CAP* (Common Agricultural Policy – France's nest egg) *costs us £15 billion* – adding to a *total annual cost of £23 billion.* No wonder we are plunged ever heavier into debt. Hence this Labour Government's cutting back and closing hospitals, post offices etc, driven by the continuous cost of EU regulations and demands, which they meet and obey without question. Why no protests, refusal to accept or seeking public support? *One wonders, are they all willing accomplices in this progressive, calculated destruction of Britain?*

Such are the methods used by GEU in revenge for our hard-won defensive victories in two German World Wars – *to reduce Britain from a World-leading Nation to a Third World Country, unable to pay our way or afford a reasonable sized Armed Defence Force, compared with her now giant Bundeswehr, second biggest in the World next to the USA.*

Once the tightly drawn net closes finally on Britain, to be confined within the German dominated EU Superstate, the once United Kingdom would be reduced to similar unit size to other members. The jealously guarded Sovereignty under the Crown and Freedom under our own laws, whereby our people cannot be held under arrest until proven guilty, will all be swept aside, with the power of Sovereign and Parliament. Those ancient rights will vanish under the rule and laws of the EU Superstate. *Britain has already been redrawn into block Regions under EU plans of Regionalisation of Europe, sweeping aside ancient boundaries and customs.*

The 1997 Amsterdam treaty gave EU control of our borders, letting in 10 million immigrants, many living in ghettoes where English is not spoken and ethics, dress and customs differ sharply. Our towns, schools and hospitals are overcrowded and often unmanageable. Robbery mayhem, bombing, shooting and injuries, murder with knives growing out of control, including school children swept into this climate of disrespect and murderous attacks brought upon us by the EU. Massive immigration caused housing problems, with deliberately low interest rates *forcing up prices to highest levels. Now the economy is being collapsed, with increasing interest rates, making house prices dive, causing negative equity. Thousands of houses being repossessed. The communist-style EU is against private ownership of property and capitalism generally. Unemployment is steadily increasing as immigration reduces wage levels.*

The cost of EU to Britain continues to rise. Now £295 billion per annum: Quangos cost £167 billion, Regulatory costs £23 billion, plus £28 billion (£56 bn contribution + £3 bn rebate return plus CAP £15 bn) per annum = £808 million every day. *Total cost of 35 years in the EU estimates £5,162 billion. Total benefits NIL* – as may be reckoned in our economy's downward slide. Think of the benefit those thousands of billions could have brought our basic industry, homes, hospitals and schools under proper management, with a well-guided Police force. *Instead this huge financial extraction plus enforced massive immigration out of control, has turned us into a Third World economy, heading for mass unemployment, loss of manufacturing, fishing and farming and near bankruptcy.*

The British Constitution versus EU Con/Treaty

Britain possesses the World's most ancient, evolved Constitution. Summarised in Halsburg's Laws of England, Vol.8. Our laws evolve continuously over the centuries, often judge-made. The Constitution limits the power of the State over the people, by providing rights and remedies for abuse. The Rule of Law defines the basis of constitutional right by which Parliament may not bind its successors. The British Constitution is the basis of the powers defining the sovereignty of Parliament, which is bound through its allegiance to the Crown and the Crown to the people.

The law and the people are supreme, not Parliament nor the Crown. In our statute law, the *rights and liberties are the birthright of the people, as proven by the Magna Carta of 1215*, which put down the usurpation of authority sought by King John, and the Declaration and Bill of Rights which dealt likewise with James II. *Since 1689 there has been no Divine Right of Kings.* The overreaching of industrialist and coal barons, was equally put down by democracy and the early trade unions – as was that of the trade union barons by Margaret Thatcher. Now we suffer from the overreaching of the European Union, with the *inherited divine right of petition to our Monarch, secured in our constitution, to achieve redress and remedy.*

We are faced with a document (Treaty) which seeks to annexe the UK (as if it were a colony) into an all-powerful European Union, which reeks of despotism. But the *Bill of Rights of 1689* declared that *"no foreign prince, person, prelate, state or potentate hath or ought to have any jurisdiction, power, superiority, pre-eminence or authority, ecclesiastical or spiritual, within the realm".* Ministers who promote the interests of the EU over the UK are breach of their oath of allegiance, and should be removed from office. Their new Law is that 'The People must not know and never discover their true situation, fearing they would rise in anger, as in the past, to evict these paid deceivers'.

Thomas Cromwell in 1533 (Act in Restraint of Appeals): "This realm of England is an Empire, governed by one Supreme Head and King. It is a sovereign state with a king who owes no submission to any other human ruler and is invested with plenary powers to give justice to his people in all causes".

In Britain power is on loan to the politicians for only 5 years, then must be returned. Without Parliament, we will cease to be a free democratic nation. Our Government must rescind the illegal Communities Act of 1972, to free us from this Federal Superstate.

The Treasured Principles of the British Constitution

(ref. John Gouriet)

Tom Paine said: *"The Constitution is made for the people, and not the government".*
1 - Sovereignty is the inalienable birthright of the people, entrusted to the Monarch and administered by Parliament which itself has no lawful authority ever to breach, surrender, lend or transfer sovereignty, except when conquered in war.
2 - No one (neither Monarch, nor Prime Minister, nor any prelate, politician, judge or public servant) is above the Statute and Common Law of the

UK that form the British Constitution (including Magna Carta of 1215, the Declaration and Bill of Rights (1688/89), Acts of Union, Succession and Settlement (1701-07) and the Coronation Oath (1689) – all codified.

3 - British Citizens have an inalienable right to be governed justly, lawfully and exclusively by their Parliament in Westminster (the Crown, the Lords Spiritual and Temporal and freely elected/replaceable representatives in the Commons) all of whom are servants of the people. Parliament's power is not supreme, but conditioned by oaths of office under the Constitution.

4 - Trial by Jury, habeas corpus and right of appeal are the inalienable right of all accused persons under British jurisdiction.

5 - Innocence is presumed unless proven guilty in Court.

6 - The British Constitution is sworn by solemn oaths of office and/or allegiance to be upheld and defended impartially in perpetuity without exception by the Monarch, ministers, politicians, judges, members of the forces, police and others in authority.

7 - No taxation is lawful without representation, nor may taxes be oppressive, unnecessary, confiscatory, or contain double tax (eg VAT on petrol tax).

8 - No fine or forfeiture before conviction by a court.

9 - The Government must always act within limits and constraints imposed by the Constitution; including the making and unmaking of law; it may not diminish or transfer its own power so to act; nor weaken ignore or override the Constitution whether to serve its own or other's ends; it may not suspend or dispense with the law; nor impose harsh or punitive law without cause.

10 - Constitutional law takes precedence over administrative law. It may be improved, or expressly repealed if not entrenched; however it may never be supplanted or repealed just by passing a new statute or administrative instrument.

11 - British Citizens may petition the Monarch if all other remedies fail,

without fear of reprisal or prosecution. The Crown is sworn by oath to protect all subjects from violation of their lawful rights and liberties, retaining the power and responsibility to ensure redress is exercisable.

12 - Guaranteed justice. There must be no undue delay in legal proceedings. Immigrants must adhere to British laws and customs. If wronged British Citizens are entitled to a remedy, and to seek redress in law. Punishment must fit the crime and must not be excessive or unusual, such as torture. Judgements must be exercised with compassion and mercy at every level.

13/18 - Rights: to be defended from our enemies; to defend self family and property by whatever reasonable means necessary; to private ownership of property and assets; to engage in any activity not specifically banned in the national interest; to associate freely or not to associate with any particular party, trade union or organisation, except those posing a threat to security and interests of the UK; to freedom of speech, writing and publication.

19 - Freedom of worship, except the Protestant Succession be maintained.

20 - The Royal Prerogative shall be exercised personally by the Sovereign on all Constitutional issues and foreign treaties. Never by Ministers on behalf of the Crown. The prerogative power is lent to the monarch by the People at Coronation for their lifetime. But PM Blair, followed by G. Brown (acting on EU instructions), sought to transfer the prerogative to Parliament, thus removing it from protection of the monarch and judiciary. But the Law Lords ruled that Parliament had acted 'outside' their power. Removal of the prerogative is Treason against the principles of our country, which protect the people against the tyranny we now suffer.

21 - Separation of Powers between Crown, Executive and legislative be invariably maintained.

22 - The Crown shall always retain the right to dissolve and open Parliament; call General Elections; refuse Royal Assent to any Bill that does not enjoy the settled will of Parliament or the interests of the nation or is unconstitutional; receive and act upon public petitions; declare war if unavoidable only in self-defence of the UK and our vital interests. Going to War lies with the Monarch for decision. NOT Parliament. An Oath of

Allegiance must be taken by anyone taking a seat in Parliament, as per the laws of the land, which this government seeks to break. Blair has been allowed to act as Dictator by ignorance deliberately propagated amongst the people of this nation. This was the culminatory act of Treason, following Heath's original lying, unlawful commitment of the United Kingdom to this unelected, improperly devised consortium behind the European Union. *It was revealed at Heath's death that he was in the service of German Intelligence, as was Roy Jenkins. Therefore his 1972 Treaty was false and illegal, as has all the furtherance of EU ever since. He was guilty of lying to the British people, committing Treason as Prime Minister. His original crime was countenanced and furthered by succeeding Leaders.*

The Traitor Within the Gates: Cicero (106-43BC): A nation can survive its fools, and even the ambitious, but it cannot survive treason from within. An enemy at the gates is less formidable, for he is known and he carries his banners openly against the city. But the traitor moves among those within the gates freely, his sly whispers rustling through all alleys, heard in the very halls of government itself. For the traitor appears no traitor; he speaks in the accents familiar to his victims, and he wears their face and their garments and he appeals to the baseness that lies deep in the hearts of all men. He rots the soul of a nation; he works secretly and unknown in the night to undermine the pillars of a city; he infects the body politic so that it can no longer resist. A murderer is less to be feared. The traitor is the plague.

Freedom under the Law: Comparison with EU
British Common Law

Law of Habeas Corpus: Precludes the possibility of detention without public hearing for more than 24 hours or, exceptionally, up to 96 hours.

Trial by Jury: Gives the defendant the right to trial by his peers i.e. members of the general public chosen at random.

Presumption of Innocence: Under British Law all are deemed to be innocent unless proven otherwise. The onus is on the prosecution to prove their case.

Double Jeopardy: Once acquitted a defendant may not be charged again with the same offence and the prosecution may not appeal.

Law of Right to Silence: Avoids the possibility of defendant being condemned by his own evidence.

Inadmissibility of Hearsay: Obviates the possibility of the defendant being found guilty on the basis of say-so evidence from absent 'witnesses'.

Withholding of Previous Convictions: Ensures that the hearing of cases brought to court are not prejudiced by the defendants previous record.

Reporting Restrictions: Whilst matters are sub judice Press reporting is limited so as not to prejudice a fair trial.

European System: has no equivalent. Persons may be arrested and held without charge for months, even years without a public hearing and without any obligation on the prosecution to exhibit evidence whilst it 'prepares its case'. Cases are heard by and justice is dispensed entirely by a career judiciary. The proclamation of a presumption of innocence in several continental constitutions does not, in practice, prevent the defendant from being treated as 'presumed guilty' and kept in prison for long periods without trial. In the event of an acquittal the prosecution may appeal for the defendant to be tried again.

No Equivalent: Prosecutors may claim that a defendant's refusal to answer questions is an admission of guilt. Reported' evidence is frequently used to obtain convictions. Defendant's record, including prosecutions pending, may be read out at the hearing. The Press are free to name names and express opinions before as well as during a trial.

Charles I said: Power without law: means no man or his property is safe. Parliament is the supreme protector of our laws which are the Birthright of the people of the UK. Parliament is bound through its allegiance to the Crown and the Crown to the people. It is bound by oath and by the statute of law. Inquisitorial practice is permitted where "reasonable suspicion" in the view of an investigating prosecution judge (with a judge of freedom). Parliament is bound by the Common Law, the custom, and by primary constitutional statutes of its predecessors. Parliament's own hand book admits this to be also the MPs code of conduct and oaths of office.

What we are now facing

A German controlled European Union, now revealed as based on the Soviet collectivist totalitarian principle (as warned by Christopher Story and myself), whose origins date back to the doctrine of Adam Weishaupt, a profligate ex-Jesuit, who founded in 1782 the "Bavarian Illuminati", which openly denied the existence of God, in favour of the devil (or fallen Angel of Light)? Weishaupt postulates (repeated by Marx in his Communist Manifesto):
1 - Abolish all monarchies and all ordered government.

2 - Abolish private property and the right of inheritance.

3 - Abolish patriotism and nationalism.

4 - Abolish the family unit, marriage, and the establishment of communal organisations.

5 - Abolish all organised religion.

They are spreading their tentacles ever wider through the EU in their aim at World Government. Corruption and fraud are widespread. EU's oft changing auditors found massive fraud so widespread that they have refused to sign off EU's accounts for the past 10 years at least. Whistle-blowers like Marta Andreason the Budget Director who, in 2005, found the EU could not account for 95% of its £66 billion budget, are simply fired for telling the truth. So they seek practitioners and officers of their own ilk, fully cooperative in cover up.

EU's 111,000 binding regulations cause such time and labour, with costing complications and such excessive paper work, that our police are desk-bound, unable to carry out their normal duties of maintaining law and order. Thousands of small businesses are forced to close, throwing thousands out of work. In addition, the 1997 Amsterdam Treaty gave EU control of immigration, resulting in tenfold increase, overcrowded cities with millions on minimum wage, supplied with houses, furniture and maintenance, but failing to relieve our own unemployed situation. Obviously this has not come by accident, but rather a carefully pre-arranged upset of our normal economic administration, to overcome any opposition they cannot buy, while assuring us that all will be well, when we are fully within the net. We will then have no worries from Parliament, which will cease to function as all will be directed from Brussels. Instead we will function with our planned 9 Regions, each with its Capital and Minister answerable direct to Brussels, where he will have to plead for necessary funds from our regular payments to our masters.

Our 153 Embassies will be closed; our Union Jack replaced by EU stars, and we shall sing 'Ode To Joy' instead of God save the Queen, who may then be transformed into Mrs Windsor. The GEU maintains that democracy is outmoded, and their communist style binds us into a better life of equality for all on lower level, except for our predestined Leaders, who must be praised and obeyed in the instructions they lay before us.

Destruction of Britain as a major leading nation

The German controlled EU plans to destroy not only Britain's economy, industry and world respect, but also her very geographical entity. Under the Regional Assemblies Development Act of 1998, began the planned Regionalisation, destroying England's ancient Counties and boundaries, sensibly arranged by wise ancestors, and replacing with ugly misshapen lumps to suit EU's secret plans, now being revealed. These 9 Regions will each be directly answerable to Brussels, (ruling out our Parliament), with taxation apportioned by EU, to whom we must also apply for our needs. A Minister will be appointed to plead for such negotiations, without the need for MPs.

A further operation, now exposed, is the surgical dissection of this once 'Great' Britain, with malice aforethought as follows: Southern areas of England, including Cornwall, Devon, Dorset, Hampshire, Sussex, Kent, Essex, Suffolk, Norfolk, will be joined to Northern France in the new Manche region, under French rule.

The English Channel to be renamed as The Channel Sea.

In addition is planned The Atlantic Region, comprising West England and Wales to be joined to Portugal and Spain, a daunting operation. Finally, a North Sea region will consist of a marriage between large parts of East and North England, and Sweden, Denmark, Germany and the Netherlands.

The name of England will disappear, as will, I presume, many of the erstwhile inhabitants, opting for freedom whilst the rest of us continue the struggle. The rump left, about the size of Wales or Jersey (whose fate we have still to learn), is envisaged to become a haven for tourists. Our farmers will become land stewards to keep the country in good shape as a tourism asset. Any plans for our long suffering fishermen are yet to be revealed. Possibly lifeboatmen to look after tourists' welfare in or on the sea.

'Tis' a sorry tale my masters, but expected and forecast by the cognoscenti, with little heed taken by the broad mass of our people, who have been kept, very carefully, in almost complete ignorance of the fate awaiting them. I did forecast much in my first edition of "Germany's Four Reichs", of her amazing recovery after final defeat in WWII, repeatedly emphasising Germany's refusal to accept defeat, and immediately rebuilding her Bundeswehr in readiness for her next attempt at conquering first Europe, then the World. With Europe in her maw without combat, one wonders at the need for over 350,000 fully armed, trained troops with the world's latest armaments, and fully sustained conscription producing some 60,000 training annually. Her old foe Britain, cunningly reduced to a mere shadow of home defence, her fighting forces spread far afield. Could she be preparing for a final direct assault, with victory now well within her grasp? Or is her gaze now fixed on wider targets?

But we are concerned with our struggle here and now for the absolute freedom which is our birthright. We have been brought low by cunning perversion of our accredited leaders, since Churchill, our last great Englishman to defy the odds mounted against us. However, the Republic of Ireland, the only country to be allowed a Referendum, has returned a resounding, decisive NO on behalf of us all, who would surely return the same verdict, were our deceitful Government to keep their promise of a Referendum.

Without 100% agreement, this latest perpetration of a Con/Treaty now fails. Yet, instead of accepting the Irish verdict as final, the deceitful EU will not take NO for an acceptable answer. They seek a way round this impasse, such as their repeated trick of forcing the refusing country to vote again and again, until they are eventually ground down to a reluctant agreement. It is now our bounden duty to gather all loyal forces to ensure acceptance of the brave Irish refusal as a final end to this attempted dictatorship of the Con/Treaty, and declare it stone dead. At the same time to seize this heaven-sent opportunity to withdraw Britain from our overlong, ruinous captivity.

The voice of our people, once raised, will not be denied. They are the real strength of Great Britain, with England, Scotland, Wales and Ireland combining in the United Kingdom. A truly unbeatable force, once roused, as in the past, in the defence of our Country and Europe, cunningly kept in the dark by these evil plotters. They seek to destroy our Country, our freedom to enjoy our own way of life, our education system, even our Union Jack, which led us in battle, as well as our National Anthem, leaving us an empty shell. So this is my cry for concerted attack on all who seek to imprison the people of this proud United Kingdom, in a ceaseless effort until we cast off the closing net of the German-led European disUnion, and win back our total Freedom and sovereignty, under our own laws and customs, brooking no interference; simply living at peace and friendly cooperation with our neighbours, safe in our island home, as voiced by our own Shakespeare:

"This fortress built by Nature for herself,
Against infection and the hand of war;
This happy breed of men, this little world,
This precious stone set in the silver sea,
Which serves it in the office of a wall
Or as a moat defensive to a house,
Against the envy of less happy lands.
This blessed plot, this earth, this realm, this England."